# METHOD OF USE

1. **Game Details**

    At the top of each page you can record:—

    Date of game

    Opponents

    Whether Home or Away — delete as appropriate

    Number of Overs (if Limited Over Game)

    League or Division concerned

    The number of Players on each side, your side first, e.g. 5 v 5; 10 v 11.

2. **Team Result**

    Delete Won, Lost or Drawn as appropriate.

    Show the margin of victory (or defeat) in the spaces provided, and the points awarded.

    Show the number of runs and wickets for both sides.

3. **Personal Record — Batting**

    Spaces provided to record interesting and important details.

    All your runs should be shown opposite "Runs" including boundaries. Show the number of 6's and 4's respectively in the spaces provided.

    Show your longest combined score with the partner concerned under "Wicket Partnership" — name and runs.

    Alongside "How Out" show how your wicket was taken; or if not out, record that.

4. **Personal Record — Bowling**

    If you are bowling, space is provided for recording your achievements opposite to the various items listed.

    The "Total Number of Bowlers" is to record how many bowled for your side (including yourself).

5. **Personal Record —Fielding**

   Provision is made for you to record the main positions in which you fielded, together with a record of what contribution you made in the field.

6. **Rating Performance**

   Rate your performance in comparison with your team. If you scored the most runs, enter 1; if any aspect was second best, enter 2 and so on.

7. **Weather and Effect on Game**

   In this section you can record the effect of the weather — including sighting — on the game; both on your game and the team result.

8. **Injuries**

   Hopefully, there will be none — to anyone in either team.

9. **Other Useful Notes**

   A section is provided for any other notes you may wish to make.

10. **Opponents**

    It may be useful to make notes on opponents' performance, particularly if it will assist you when you next play them. Special pages are provided at the rear of this book.

11. **Season's Performance**

    At the rear of the book is a section for summarising your performance for the season, including wickets you take as bowler or fielder.

## 12. Team Ranking for Season

This section enables you to record your relative position in comparison with other team players for each of the three sections separately, Batting, Bowling and Fielding.

## 13. Highlights

Also included are special sections to record highlights e.g. trophies, etc. — one section for personal highlights and one for team highlights.

Date ........................................20..... v. ............................................ C.C. Home/Away
League ........................... Division ............ Overs ............ Players ..............

## TEAM RESULT:

Won/Lost/Drawn by .................. Runs/by .................. Wickets .................. Points
Our Runs ............... Wickets ............... Their Runs ............... Wickets ...............

## PERSONAL RECORD

| Batting | Rating | Bowling | Rating |
|---|---|---|---|
| Batting Order ........................ | | Number of Overs ...................... | |
| Runs ...................................... | | Maiden Overs ........................ | |
| Number of 6's ........................ | | Wickets ................................. | |
| Number of 4's ........................ | | Runs ..................................... | |
| Wicket Partnership ................ | | Extras .................................... | |
|     Name ................................ | |     No Balls ........................... | |
|     Runs ................................. | |     Wides .............................. | |
| Number of Overs ................... | |     Byes ................................ | |
| Number balls faced ............... | |     Leg Byes ......................... | |
| How out ................................ | | Bowling Average ..................... | |
| **Fielding** | | Analysis of Wickets Taken ..... | |
| Main Positions ...................... | |     Bowled ............................ | |
| ............................................... | |     Caught ............................ | |
| Catches ................................ | |     Caught & Bowled ............ | |
| Run out ................................. | |     L.B.W. ............................. | |
| *Stumped ............................. | |     Other .............................. | |
| *Byes .................................... | | | |
| *If Keeping Wicket | | Total Number of Bowlers ....... | |

## NOTES

Weather and Effect on Game

Injuries

Other Useful Notes

Date ........................................20..... v. ........................................ C.C. Home/Away
League ................................ Division ............. Overs ............. Players ...............

## TEAM RESULT:

Won/Lost/Drawn by .................. Runs/by .................. Wickets .................. Points
Our Runs ............... Wickets ............... Their Runs ............... Wickets ...............

## PERSONAL RECORD

| Batting | Rating | Bowling | Rating |
|---|---|---|---|

Batting Order ........................ ............... | Number of Overs ........................ ...............
Runs .................................... ............... | Maiden Overs ........................... ...............
Number of 6's ....................... ............... | Wickets ..................................... ...............
Number of 4's ....................... ............... | Runs ......................................... ...............
Wicket Partnership ............... ............... | Extras ....................................... ...............
    Name ........................... ............... |     No Balls ............................ ...............
    Runs ............................ ............... |     Wides ................................ ...............
Number of Overs ................... ............... |     Byes .................................. ...............
Number balls faced ............... ............... |     Leg Byes ........................... ...............
How out ................................ ............... | Bowling Average ..................... ...............

**Fielding** | Analysis of Wickets Taken ..... ...............

Main Positions ...................... ............... |     Bowled ............................... ...............
    ........................................ ............... |     Caught ............................... ...............
Catches ................................ ............... |     Caught & Bowled .............. ...............
Run out ................................. ............... |     L.B.W. ................................ ...............
*Stumped ............................. ............... |     Other ................................. ...............
*Byes ................................... ............... |
*If Keeping Wicket | Total Number of Bowlers ....... ...............

## NOTES

Weather and Effect on Game

Injuries

Other Useful Notes

Date .........................20..... v. ........................ C.C. Home/Away
League ............................... Division ............ Overs ............ Players ............

## TEAM RESULT:

Won/Lost/Drawn by ................. Runs/by ................. Wickets ................ Points
Our Runs .............. Wickets ............... Their Runs ............... Wickets ..............

## PERSONAL RECORD

| Batting | Rating | Bowling | Rating |
|---|---|---|---|
| Batting Order ........................... | | Number of Overs ........................... | |
| Runs ................................................ | | Maiden Overs ............................... | |
| Number of 6's ............................. | | Wickets ........................................... | |
| Number of 4's ............................. | | Runs ................................................ | |
| Wicket Partnership ..................... | | Extras ............................................. | |
|    Name ........................................... | |    No Balls ..................................... | |
|    Runs ............................................. | |    Wides ......................................... | |
| Number of Overs ........................ | |    Byes ............................................ | |
| Number balls faced .................... | |    Leg Byes .................................... | |
| How out ........................................ | | Bowling Average ......................... | |
| **Fielding** | | Analysis of Wickets Taken ....... | |
| Main Positions ............................ | |    Bowled ....................................... | |
| ............................................ | |    Caught ........................................ | |
| Catches ......................................... | |    Caught & Bowled ..................... | |
| Run out ......................................... | |    L.B.W. .......................................... | |
| *Stumped ..................................... | |    Other ........................................... | |
| *Byes .............................................. | | | |
| *If Keeping Wicket | | Total Number of Bowlers ............ | |

## NOTES

Weather and Effect on Game

Injuries

Other Useful Notes

Date ........................20..... v. ........................................ C.C. Home/Away
League ............................ Division ............ Overs ............ Players ..............

## TEAM RESULT:

Won/Lost/Drawn by .................. Runs/by ................. Wickets ................. Points
Our Runs ............... Wickets ............... Their Runs ............... Wickets ..............

## PERSONAL RECORD

| Batting | Rating | Bowling | Rating |
|---|---|---|---|
| Batting Order ................ | | Number of Overs ................ | |
| Runs ................ | | Maiden Overs ................ | |
| Number of 6's ................ | | Wickets ................ | |
| Number of 4's ................ | | Runs ................ | |
| Wicket Partnership ................ | | Extras ................ | |
|     Name ................ | |     No Balls ................ | |
|     Runs ................ | |     Wides ................ | |
| Number of Overs ................ | |     Byes ................ | |
| Number balls faced ................ | |     Leg Byes ................ | |
| How out ................ | | Bowling Average ................ | |
| **Fielding** | | Analysis of Wickets Taken ........ | |
| Main Positions ................ | |     Bowled ................ | |
| ................ | |     Caught ................ | |
| Catches ................ | |     Caught & Bowled ................ | |
| Run out ................ | |     L.B.W. ................ | |
| *Stumped ................ | |     Other ................ | |
| *Byes ................ | | | |
| *If Keeping Wicket | | Total Number of Bowlers ........ | |

## NOTES

Weather and Effect on Game
Injuries
Other Useful Notes

Date ........................20..... v. ........................ C.C. Home/Away
League ................... Division ............ Overs ............ Players ...........

## TEAM RESULT:

Won/Lost/Drawn by .................. Runs/by ................. Wickets ................ Points
Our Runs ............... Wickets ............... Their Runs ............... Wickets ...............

## PERSONAL RECORD

| Batting | Rating | Bowling | Rating |
|---|---|---|---|
| Batting Order ........................... | | Number of Overs ........................... | |
| Runs ........................................ | | Maiden Overs ........................... | |
| Number of 6's ........................... | | Wickets ........................... | |
| Number of 4's ........................... | | Runs ........................... | |
| Wicket Partnership ................. | | Extras ........................... | |
|     Name ................................. | |     No Balls ........................... | |
|     Runs ................................. | |     Wides ........................... | |
| Number of Overs ........................... | |     Byes ........................... | |
| Number balls faced .................... | |     Leg Byes ........................... | |
| How out ........................... | | Bowling Average ........................... | |
| **Fielding** | | Analysis of Wickets Taken ............... | |
| Main Positions ........................... | |     Bowled ........................... | |
| ........................... | |     Caught ........................... | |
| Catches ........................... | |     Caught & Bowled ........................... | |
| Run out ........................... | |     L.B.W. ........................... | |
| *Stumped ........................... | |     Other ........................... | |
| *Byes ........................... | | | |
| *If Keeping Wicket | | Total Number of Bowlers ............... | |

## NOTES

Weather and Effect on Game

Injuries

Other Useful Notes

Date ........................................20..... v. ........................................ C.C. Home/Away
League ................................ Division ............. Overs ............. Players ..............

---

## TEAM RESULT:

Won/Lost/Drawn by .................. Runs/by .................. Wickets .................. Points
Our Runs ............... Wickets ............... Their Runs ............... Wickets ...............

---

## PERSONAL RECORD

| Batting | Rating | Bowling | Rating |
|---|---|---|---|
| Batting Order ........................... | | Number of Overs ............................... | |
| Runs ......................................... | | Maiden Overs .................................... | |
| Number of 6's ........................... | | Wickets ............................................. | |
| Number of 4's ........................... | | Runs ................................................. | |
| Wicket Partnership ............................ | | Extras ............................................... | |
|     Name ............................................ | |     No Balls ........................................ | |
|     Runs ............................................. | |     Wides ............................................. | |
| Number of Overs ............................. | |     Byes ............................................... | |
| Number balls faced ....................... | |     Leg Byes ........................................ | |
| How out ...................................... | | Bowling Average ............................... | |
| **Fielding** | | Analysis of Wickets Taken ................... | |
| Main Positions ............................. | |     Bowled ........................................... | |
| ................................................... | |     Caught ............................................ | |
| Catches ...................................... | |     Caught & Bowled ............................ | |
| Run out ....................................... | |     L.B.W. ............................................. | |
| *Stumped ................................... | |     Other ............................................... | |
| *Byes ......................................... | | | |
| *If Keeping Wicket | | Total Number of Bowlers ..................... | |

## NOTES

Weather and Effect on Game

Injuries

Other Useful Notes

Date ........................................20..... v. ........................................ C.C. Home/Away
League ................................ Division ............ Overs ............ Players ..............

## TEAM RESULT:

Won/Lost/Drawn by .................. Runs/by .................. Wickets ................. Points
Our Runs ............... Wickets ............... Their Runs ............... Wickets ...............

## PERSONAL RECORD

| Batting | Rating | Bowling | Rating |
|---|---|---|---|
| Batting Order ........................................ | | Number of Overs ........................................ | |
| Runs ........................................ | | Maiden Overs ........................................ | |
| Number of 6's ........................................ | | Wickets ........................................ | |
| Number of 4's ........................................ | | Runs ........................................ | |
| Wicket Partnership ........................................ | | Extras ........................................ | |
| Name ........................................ | | No Balls ........................................ | |
| Runs ........................................ | | Wides ........................................ | |
| Number of Overs ........................................ | | Byes ........................................ | |
| Number balls faced ........................................ | | Leg Byes ........................................ | |
| How out ........................................ | | Bowling Average ........................................ | |
| **Fielding** | | Analysis of Wickets Taken ........................................ | |
| Main Positions ........................................ | | Bowled ........................................ | |
| ........................................ | | Caught ........................................ | |
| Catches ........................................ | | Caught & Bowled ........................................ | |
| Run out ........................................ | | L.B.W. ........................................ | |
| *Stumped ........................................ | | Other ........................................ | |
| *Byes ........................................ | | | |
| *If Keeping Wicket | | Total Number of Bowlers ........................................ | |

## NOTES

Weather and Effect on Game

Injuries

Other Useful Notes

Date ..............................20..... v. ..................................... C.C. Home/Away
League ................................ Division ............ Overs ............ Players ..............

---

## TEAM RESULT:

Won/Lost/Drawn by .................. Runs/by .................. Wickets .................. Points
Our Runs ............... Wickets ............... Their Runs ............... Wickets ...............

---

## PERSONAL RECORD

| Batting | Rating | Bowling | Rating |
|---|---|---|---|

**Batting** | Rating
Batting Order .....................................
Runs ....................................................
Number of 6's ...................................
Number of 4's ...................................
Wicket Partnership ............................
    Name ............................................
    Runs .............................................
Number of Overs ...............................
Number balls faced ..........................
How out .............................................

**Fielding**
Main Positions ..................................
.............................................................
Catches ..............................................
Run out ..............................................
*Stumped ..........................................
*Byes .................................................
*If Keeping Wicket

**Bowling** | Rating
Number of Overs ...............................
Maiden Overs ...................................
Wickets ...............................................
Runs ....................................................
Extras .................................................
    No Balls ......................................
    Wides ...........................................
    Byes ..............................................
    Leg Byes ......................................
Bowling Average ...............................
Analysis of Wickets Taken ..................
    Bowled .........................................
    Caught ..........................................
    Caught & Bowled .......................
    L.B.W. ...........................................
    Other .............................................
Total Number of Bowlers ....................

## NOTES

Weather and Effect on Game

Injuries

Other Useful Notes

Date .................................20..... v. ....................................... C.C. Home/Away
League ................................ Division ............. Overs ............. Players ..............

---

## TEAM RESULT:

Won/Lost/Drawn by .................. Runs/by .................. Wickets .................. Points
Our Runs ............... Wickets ................ Their Runs ............... Wickets ...............

---

## PERSONAL RECORD

| Batting | Rating | Bowling | Rating |
|---|---|---|---|
| Batting Order ........................... | | Number of Overs ........................... | |
| Runs ........................................ | | Maiden Overs ............................... | |
| Number of 6's ........................... | | Wickets ....................................... | |
| Number of 4's ........................... | | Runs ........................................... | |
| Wicket Partnership .................... | | Extras ......................................... | |
|     Name ............................... | |     No Balls ............................... | |
|     Runs ................................ | |     Wides .................................. | |
| Number of Overs ....................... | |     Byes ................................... | |
| Number balls faced ................... | |     Leg Byes ............................. | |
| How out ................................... | | Bowling Average ......................... | |
| **Fielding** | | Analysis of Wickets Taken .......... | |
| Main Positions .......................... | |     Bowled ................................ | |
| .................................................. | |     Caught ................................ | |
| Catches ..................................... | |     Caught & Bowled ................ | |
| Run out .................................... | |     L.B.W. ................................. | |
| *Stumped ................................. | |     Other ................................... | |
| *Byes ........................................ | | | |
| *If Keeping Wicket | | Total Number of Bowlers ............ | |

## NOTES

Weather and Effect on Game

Injuries

Other Useful Notes

Date ........................................20..... v. ........................................ C.C. Home/Away
League ................................. Division ............. Overs ............. Players ..............

## TEAM RESULT:

Won/Lost/Drawn by ................. Runs/by ................. Wickets ................. Points
Our Runs ............... Wickets ................ Their Runs ............... Wickets ...............

## PERSONAL RECORD

| Batting | Rating | Bowling | Rating |
|---|---|---|---|
| Batting Order ................................... | | Number of Overs ................................ | |
| Runs ................................................... | | Maiden Overs ..................................... | |
| Number of 6's ................................... | | Wickets ............................................... | |
| Number of 4's ................................... | | Runs ................................................... | |
| Wicket Partnership ............................ | | Extras ................................................. | |
|     Name ............................................ | |     No Balls ........................................ | |
|     Runs ............................................. | |     Wides ............................................ | |
| Number of Overs ............................... | |     Byes .............................................. | |
| Number balls faced ........................... | |     Leg Byes ....................................... | |
| How out ............................................ | | Bowling Average ................................ | |
| **Fielding** | | Analysis of Wickets Taken ................ | |
| Main Positions .................................. | |     Bowled ........................................... | |
| ........................................ | |     Caught ........................................... | |
| Catches ............................................. | |     Caught & Bowled ......................... | |
| Run out ............................................. | |     L.B.W. ............................................ | |
| *Stumped .......................................... | |     Other .............................................. | |
| *Byes ................................................. | | | |
| *If Keeping Wicket | | Total Number of Bowlers ................... | |

## NOTES

Weather and Effect on Game

Injuries

Other Useful Notes

Date ........................................20..... v. ........................................ C.C. Home/Away
League ................................ Division ............ Overs ............ Players ...............

## TEAM RESULT:

Won/Lost/Drawn by .................. Runs/by .................. Wickets .................. Points
Our Runs ............... Wickets ................ Their Runs ............... Wickets ...............

## PERSONAL RECORD

| Batting | Rating | Bowling | Rating |
|---|---|---|---|
| Batting Order ........................................ | | Number of Overs ........................................ | |
| Runs ........................................ | | Maiden Overs ........................................ | |
| Number of 6's ........................................ | | Wickets ........................................ | |
| Number of 4's ........................................ | | Runs ........................................ | |
| Wicket Partnership ........................... | | Extras ........................................ | |
|     Name ........................................ | |     No Balls ........................................ | |
|     Runs ........................................ | |     Wides ........................................ | |
| Number of Overs ........................................ | |     Byes ........................................ | |
| Number balls faced ........................... | |     Leg Byes ........................................ | |
| How out ........................................ | | Bowling Average ........................................ | |
| **Fielding** | | Analysis of Wickets Taken .................. | |
| Main Positions ........................................ | |     Bowled ........................................ | |
| ........................................ | |     Caught ........................................ | |
| Catches ........................................ | |     Caught & Bowled ........................ | |
| Run out ........................................ | |     L.B.W. ........................................ | |
| *Stumped ........................................ | |     Other ........................................ | |
| *Byes ........................................ | | | |
| *If Keeping Wicket | | Total Number of Bowlers ................. | |

## NOTES

Weather and Effect on Game

Injuries

Other Useful Notes

Date ........................................20..... v. ........................................ C.C. Home/Away
League .................................. Division ............. Overs ............. Players ..............

---

## TEAM RESULT:

Won/Lost/Drawn by .................. Runs/by .................. Wickets .................. Points
Our Runs ............... Wickets ............... Their Runs ............... Wickets ...............

---

## PERSONAL RECORD

| Batting | Rating | Bowling | Rating |
|---|---|---|---|
| Batting Order ..................................... | | Number of Overs ..................................... | |
| Runs ..................................................... | | Maiden Overs ........................................ | |
| Number of 6's ..................................... | | Wickets ................................................. | |
| Number of 4's ..................................... | | Runs ...................................................... | |
| Wicket Partnership ............................ | | Extras .................................................... | |
|     Name ........................................... | |     No Balls ........................................ | |
|     Runs ............................................. | |     Wides ............................................ | |
| Number of Overs ................................ | |     Byes .............................................. | |
| Number balls faced ............................ | |     Leg Byes ....................................... | |
| How out ............................................... | | Bowling Average .................................. | |
| **Fielding** | | Analysis of Wickets Taken ................ | |
| Main Positions .................................... | |     Bowled ......................................... | |
| ...................................... | |     Caught ......................................... | |
| Catches ................................................ | |     Caught & Bowled ....................... | |
| Run out ................................................ | |     L.B.W. .......................................... | |
| *Stumped ............................................. | |     Other ............................................ | |
| *Byes .................................................... | | | |
| *If Keeping Wicket | | Total Number of Bowlers .................... | |

## NOTES

Weather and Effect on Game

Injuries

Other Useful Notes

Date ........................................20..... v. ........................................ C.C. Home/Away

League ................................ Division ............ Overs ............ Players ..............

## TEAM RESULT:

Won/Lost/Drawn by ................. Runs/by ................. Wickets ................. Points

Our Runs .............. Wickets ............... Their Runs ............... Wickets ...............

## PERSONAL RECORD

| Batting | Rating | Bowling | Rating |
|---|---|---|---|
| Batting Order ........................ | | Number of Overs ..................... | |
| Runs ................................... | | Maiden Overs ......................... | |
| Number of 6's ........................ | | Wickets ................................. | |
| Number of 4's ........................ | | Runs ..................................... | |
| Wicket Partnership ................. | | Extras ................................... | |
|     Name ............................. | |     No Balls ........................... | |
|     Runs .............................. | |     Wides .............................. | |
| Number of Overs ..................... | |     Byes ................................ | |
| Number balls faced ................. | |     Leg Byes ......................... | |
| How out ................................ | | Bowling Average .................... | |
| **Fielding** | | Analysis of Wickets Taken ...... | |
| Main Positions ....................... | |     Bowled ............................. | |
| ................................ | |     Caught .............................. | |
| Catches ................................ | |     Caught & Bowled ............... | |
| Run out ................................ | |     L.B.W. .............................. | |
| *Stumped ............................. | |     Other ................................ | |
| *Byes .................................... | | | |
| *If Keeping Wicket | | Total Number of Bowlers ....... | |

## NOTES

Weather and Effect on Game

Injuries

Other Useful Notes

Date ........................................20..... v. ...................................... C.C. Home/Away
League ................................ Division ............ Overs ............ Players ..............

---

## TEAM RESULT:

Won/Lost/Drawn by ................. Runs/by ................. Wickets ................. Points
Our Runs ............... Wickets ............... Their Runs ............... Wickets ...............

---

## PERSONAL RECORD

| Batting | Rating | Bowling | Rating |
|---|---|---|---|
| Batting Order ................................... | | Number of Overs ................................ | |
| Runs ................................................... | | Maiden Overs ...................................... | |
| Number of 6's ................................... | | Wickets ................................................ | |
| Number of 4's ................................... | | Runs ..................................................... | |
| Wicket Partnership ........................... | | Extras .................................................. | |
| Name ................................... | | No Balls ................................... | |
| Runs ................................... | | Wides ...................................... | |
| Number of Overs ............................. | | Byes ....................................... | |
| Number balls faced ......................... | | Leg Byes ................................ | |
| How out ............................................ | | Bowling Average ............................... | |
| **Fielding** | | Analysis of Wickets Taken ............... | |
| Main Positions ................................. | | Bowled ................................... | |
| ................................. | | Caught ................................... | |
| Catches ............................................. | | Caught & Bowled ...................... | |
| Run out ............................................. | | L.B.W. ..................................... | |
| *Stumped ......................................... | | Other ...................................... | |
| *Byes ................................................ | | | |
| *If Keeping Wicket | | Total Number of Bowlers .................... | |

---

## NOTES

Weather and Effect on Game

Injuries

Other Useful Notes

Date ........................................20..... v. ....................................... C.C. Home/Away
League ................................ Division ............. Overs ............. Players ..............

## TEAM RESULT:

Won/Lost/Drawn by .................. Runs/by .................. Wickets .................. Points
Our Runs ............... Wickets ................ Their Runs ............... Wickets ...............

## PERSONAL RECORD

| Batting | Rating | Bowling | Rating |
|---|---|---|---|
| Batting Order ........................ | | Number of Overs ....................... | |
| Runs ........................................ | | Maiden Overs ........................... | |
| Number of 6's ........................ | | Wickets ..................................... | |
| Number of 4's ........................ | | Runs ......................................... | |
| Wicket Partnership ............... | | Extras ....................................... | |
|     Name ............................. | |     No Balls ............................ | |
|     Runs ............................... | |     Wides ................................. | |
| Number of Overs .................. | |     Byes ................................... | |
| Number balls faced ............. | |     Leg Byes ............................ | |
| How out .................................. | | Bowling Average ....................... | |
| **Fielding** | | Analysis of Wickets Taken ..... | |
| Main Positions ....................... | |     Bowled ............................... | |
| ................................... | |     Caught ............................... | |
| Catches .................................. | |     Caught & Bowled .............. | |
| Run out .................................. | |     L.B.W. ................................ | |
| *Stumped .............................. | |     Other ................................. | |
| *Byes ..................................... | | | |
| *If Keeping Wicket | | Total Number of Bowlers ....... | |

## NOTES

Weather and Effect on Game

Injuries

Other Useful Notes

Date ..................................20..... v. ...................................... C.C. Home/Away
League ................................ Division ............. Overs ............. Players ...............

## TEAM RESULT:

Won/Lost/Drawn by .................. Runs/by .................. Wickets .................. Points
Our Runs ............... Wickets ............... Their Runs ............... Wickets ...............

## PERSONAL RECORD

| Batting | Rating | Bowling | Rating |
|---|---|---|---|

**Batting**

Batting Order .......................................
Runs .................................................
Number of 6's ....................................
Number of 4's ....................................
Wicket Partnership ...........................
    Name .........................................
    Runs ..........................................
Number of Overs ..............................
Number balls faced ..........................
How out ............................................

**Fielding**

Main Positions .................................
..............................
Catches ............................................
Run out ............................................
*Stumped .........................................
*Byes ................................................
*If Keeping Wicket

**Bowling**

Number of Overs ..............................
Maiden Overs ...................................
Wickets .............................................
Runs .................................................
Extras ...............................................
    No Balls .....................................
    Wides ........................................
    Byes ..........................................
    Leg Byes ...................................
Bowling Average ..............................
Analysis of Wickets Taken ...............
    Bowled ......................................
    Caught .......................................
    Caught & Bowled .......................
    L.B.W. ........................................
    Other .........................................
Total Number of Bowlers ..................

## NOTES

Weather and Effect on Game

Injuries

Other Useful Notes

Date ............................................20..... v. ......................................... C.C. Home/Away
League ................................. Division ............. Overs ............. Players ...............

## TEAM RESULT:

Won/Lost/Drawn by .................. Runs/by .................. Wickets .................. Points
Our Runs ............... Wickets ...............   Their Runs ............... Wickets ...............

## PERSONAL RECORD

| Batting | Rating | Bowling | Rating |
|---|---|---|---|

Batting Order ....................................  Number of Overs ..............................
Runs ..................................................  Maiden Overs ...................................
Number of 6's ...................................  Wickets .............................................
Number of 4's ...................................  Runs ..................................................
Wicket Partnership ..........................  Extras ................................................
    Name ........................................      No Balls ......................................
    Runs ..........................................      Wides ..........................................
Number of Overs ...............................      Byes .............................................
Number balls faced ...........................      Leg Byes ......................................
How out .............................................  Bowling Average .............................

**Fielding**                                        Analysis of Wickets Taken ..............
Main Positions .................................       Bowled ........................................
.................................................               Caught .........................................
Catches ............................................       Caught & Bowled .........................
Run out ............................................        L.B.W. ..........................................
*Stumped ..........................................        Other ............................................
*Byes .................................................
*If Keeping Wicket                                  Total Number of Bowlers ..................

## NOTES

Weather and Effect on Game

Injuries

Other Useful Notes

Date .................................20..... v. ....................................... C.C. Home/Away
League ................................ Division ............. Overs ............. Players ...............

---

## TEAM RESULT:

Won/Lost/Drawn by .................. Runs/by ................. Wickets .................. Points
Our Runs ............... Wickets ...............   Their Runs ............... Wickets ...............

---

## PERSONAL RECORD

| Batting | Rating | Bowling | Rating |
|---|---|---|---|

Batting Order ......................................       Number of Overs .................................
Runs ..................................................    Maiden Overs ....................................
Number of 6's ....................................        Wickets ..............................................
Number of 4's ....................................        Runs ..................................................
Wicket Partnership ...........................            Extras ................................................
    Name ..........................................             No Balls ......................................
    Runs ............................................             Wides ..........................................
Number of Overs ................................             Byes .............................................
Number balls faced ...........................              Leg Byes .....................................
How out .............................................     Bowling Average ..............................

**Fielding**                                              Analysis of Wickets Taken .................
Main Positions ...................................           Bowled ..........................................
    ..............................................                Caught ..........................................
Catches ..............................................        Caught & Bowled .......................
Run out .............................................         L.B.W. ...........................................
*Stumped ..........................................           Other .............................................
*Byes .................................................
*If Keeping Wicket                                        Total Number of Bowlers ..................

---

## NOTES

Weather and Effect on Game

Injuries

Other Useful Notes

Date ........................................20..... v. ........................................ C.C. Home/Away
League ................................ Division ............. Overs ............ Players .............

## TEAM RESULT:

Won/Lost/Drawn by .................. Runs/by .................. Wickets .................. Points
Our Runs ................ Wickets ................ Their Runs ................ Wickets ................

## PERSONAL RECORD

| **Batting** | Rating | **Bowling** | Rating |
|---|---|---|---|
| Batting Order ........................................ | | Number of Overs ........................... | |
| Runs ....................................................... | | Maiden Overs ................................. | |
| Number of 6's ....................................... | | Wickets ............................................. | |
| Number of 4's ....................................... | | Runs ................................................... | |
| Wicket Partnership ........................... | | Extras ................................................. | |
| Name ....................................... | | No Balls ................................. | |
| Runs ......................................... | | Wides ..................................... | |
| Number of Overs ............................... | | Byes ....................................... | |
| Number balls faced ........................... | | Leg Byes ............................... | |
| How out ................................................ | | Bowling Average ........................... | |
| **Fielding** | | Analysis of Wickets Taken ............... | |
| Main Positions .................................... | | Bowled ................................... | |
| ..................................... | | Caught ................................... | |
| Catches ................................................. | | Caught & Bowled ................. | |
| Run out ................................................. | | L.B.W. ..................................... | |
| *Stumped ............................................. | | Other ..................................... | |
| *Byes ..................................................... | | | |
| *If Keeping Wicket | | Total Number of Bowlers .............. | |

## NOTES

Weather and Effect on Game

Injuries

Other Useful Notes

Date ........................................20..... v. ........................................ C.C. Home/Away
League ................................. Division ............. Overs ............. Players ...............

---

## TEAM RESULT:

Won/Lost/Drawn by .................. Runs/by .................. Wickets .................. Points
Our Runs ............... Wickets ............... Their Runs ............... Wickets ...............

---

## PERSONAL RECORD

| Batting | Rating | Bowling | Rating |
|---|---|---|---|
| Batting Order .......................................... | | Number of Overs ........................... | |
| Runs ............................................ | | Maiden Overs ................................ | |
| Number of 6's ................................. | | Wickets ........................................ | |
| Number of 4's ................................. | | Runs ............................................. | |
| Wicket Partnership ......................... | | Extras ........................................... | |
|     Name ...................................... | |     No Balls ............................... | |
|     Runs ....................................... | |     Wides ................................... | |
| Number of Overs ........................... | |     Byes ...................................... | |
| Number balls faced ....................... | |     Leg Byes ............................. | |
| How out ........................................... | | Bowling Average ........................... | |
| **Fielding** | | Analysis of Wickets Taken ............ | |
| Main Positions .............................. | |     Bowled .................................. | |
| ................................. | |     Caught ................................... | |
| Catches .......................................... | |     Caught & Bowled ................. | |
| Run out .......................................... | |     L.B.W. .................................. | |
| *Stumped ....................................... | |     Other .................................... | |
| *Byes .............................................. | | | |
| *If Keeping Wicket | | Total Number of Bowlers .............. | |

## NOTES

Weather and Effect on Game

Injuries

Other Useful Notes

Date ............................................20..... v. ........................................ C.C. Home/Away
League ................................ Division ............. Overs ............. Players ..............

## TEAM RESULT:

Won/Lost/Drawn by .................. Runs/by .................. Wickets .................. Points
Our Runs ................ Wickets ................ Their Runs ................ Wickets ................

## PERSONAL RECORD

| **Batting** | Rating | **Bowling** | Rating |
|---|---|---|---|
| Batting Order ................................. | | Number of Overs ............................. | |
| Runs .............................................. | | Maiden Overs ................................. | |
| Number of 6's ................................. | | Wickets .......................................... | |
| Number of 4's ................................. | | Runs ............................................... | |
| Wicket Partnership .......................... | | Extras ............................................. | |
|     Name ........................................ | |     No Balls .................................... | |
|     Runs ......................................... | |     Wides ........................................ | |
| Number of Overs ............................. | |     Byes .......................................... | |
| Number balls faced ......................... | |     Leg Byes .................................... | |
| How out .......................................... | | Bowling Average ............................. | |
| **Fielding** | | Analysis of Wickets Taken ............... | |
| Main Positions ................................ | |     Bowled ...................................... | |
| ....................................... | |     Caught ....................................... | |
| Catches ........................................... | |     Caught & Bowled ....................... | |
| Run out ........................................... | |     L.B.W. ........................................ | |
| *Stumped ....................................... | |     Other ......................................... | |
| *Byes .............................................. | | | |
| *If Keeping Wicket | | Total Number of Bowlers ................ | |

## NOTES

Weather and Effect on Game

Injuries

Other Useful Notes

Date ........................................20..... v. ............................................ C.C. Home/Away
League ................................. Division ............. Overs ............. Players ..............

## TEAM RESULT:

Won/Lost/Drawn by .................. Runs/by .................. Wickets .................. Points
Our Runs ............... Wickets ............... Their Runs ............... Wickets ...............

## PERSONAL RECORD

| Batting | Rating | Bowling | Rating |
|---|---|---|---|
| Batting Order ..................................... | | Number of Overs ............................... | |
| Runs ................................................... | | Maiden Overs ..................................... | |
| Number of 6's ..................................... | | Wickets ................................................ | |
| Number of 4's ..................................... | | Runs .................................................... | |
| Wicket Partnership ............................ | | Extras .................................................. | |
|     Name ............................................. | |     No Balls ........................................... | |
|     Runs .............................................. | |     Wides ............................................... | |
| Number of Overs ............................... | |     Byes ................................................. | |
| Number balls faced ........................... | |     Leg Byes .......................................... | |
| How out .............................................. | | Bowling Average ............................... | |
| **Fielding** | | Analysis of Wickets Taken ................ | |
| Main Positions .................................. | |     Bowled ............................................. | |
| ..................................... | |     Caught .............................................. | |
| Catches .............................................. | |     Caught & Bowled ......................... | |
| Run out ............................................... | |     L.B.W. ................................................ | |
| *Stumped ........................................... | |     Other ................................................. | |
| *Byes ................................................... | | | |
| *If Keeping Wicket | | Total Number of Bowlers .................... | |

## NOTES

Weather and Effect on Game

Injuries

Other Useful Notes

Date ........................................20..... v. ........................................ C.C. Home/Away
League ................................ Division ............. Overs ............. Players ..............

## TEAM RESULT:

Won/Lost/Drawn by .................. Runs/by .................. Wickets .................. Points
Our Runs ............... Wickets ............... Their Runs ............... Wickets ...............

## PERSONAL RECORD

| **Batting** | Rating | **Bowling** | Rating |
|---|---|---|---|

Batting Order ........................................
Runs ........................................
Number of 6's ........................................
Number of 4's ........................................
Wicket Partnership ........................................
    Name ........................................
    Runs ........................................
Number of Overs ........................................
Number balls faced ........................................
How out ........................................

**Fielding**

Main Positions ........................................
........................................
Catches ........................................
Run out ........................................
*Stumped ........................................
*Byes ........................................
*If Keeping Wicket

Number of Overs ........................................
Maiden Overs ........................................
Wickets ........................................
Runs ........................................
Extras ........................................
    No Balls ........................................
    Wides ........................................
    Byes ........................................
    Leg Byes ........................................
Bowling Average ........................................
Analysis of Wickets Taken ..................
    Bowled ........................................
    Caught ........................................
    Caught & Bowled ........................................
    L.B.W. ........................................
    Other ........................................

Total Number of Bowlers ..................

## NOTES

Weather and Effect on Game

Injuries

Other Useful Notes

Date .................................20..... v. ....................................... C.C. Home/Away
League ............................... Division ............. Overs ............. Players ...............

## TEAM RESULT:

Won/Lost/Drawn by ................. Runs/by ................. Wickets ................. Points
Our Runs .............. Wickets ............... Their Runs ............... Wickets ...............

## PERSONAL RECORD

| Batting | Rating | Bowling | Rating |
|---|---|---|---|
| Batting Order ............................... |  | Number of Overs ............................... |  |
| Runs ............................................. |  | Maiden Overs ................................. |  |
| Number of 6's ............................... |  | Wickets .......................................... |  |
| Number of 4's ............................... |  | Runs ............................................... |  |
| Wicket Partnership ........................ |  | Extras ............................................. |  |
|     Name ..................................... |  |     No Balls ..................................... |  |
|     Runs ...................................... |  |     Wides ......................................... |  |
| Number of Overs ........................... |  |     Byes ........................................... |  |
| Number balls faced ....................... |  |     Leg Byes .................................... |  |
| How out ......................................... |  | Bowling Average ............................ |  |
| **Fielding** |  | Analysis of Wickets Taken ............. |  |
| Main Positions .............................. |  |     Bowled ....................................... |  |
| ........................................ |  |     Caught ....................................... |  |
| Catches .......................................... |  |     Caught & Bowled ....................... |  |
| Run out .......................................... |  |     L.B.W. ........................................ |  |
| *Stumped ....................................... |  |     Other .......................................... |  |
| *Byes ............................................. |  |  |  |
| *If Keeping Wicket |  | Total Number of Bowlers .................. |  |

## NOTES

Weather and Effect on Game

Injuries

Other Useful Notes

Date ........................................20..... v. .......................................... C.C. Home/Away
League ................................. Division ............. Overs ............. Players ...............

## TEAM RESULT:

Won/Lost/Drawn by .................. Runs/by .................. Wickets .................. Points
Our Runs ............... Wickets ............... Their Runs ............... Wickets ...............

## PERSONAL RECORD

| **Batting** | Rating | **Bowling** | Rating |
|---|---|---|---|
| Batting Order ....................................... | | Number of Overs ..................................... | |
| Runs ....................................................... | | Maiden Overs ......................................... | |
| Number of 6's ...................................... | | Wickets .................................................... | |
| Number of 4's ...................................... | | Runs ........................................................ | |
| Wicket Partnership ............................ | | Extras ...................................................... | |
|     Name .................................................. | |     No Balls ........................................... | |
|     Runs .................................................... | |     Wides ................................................ | |
| Number of Overs ................................. | |     Byes ................................................... | |
| Number balls faced ........................... | |     Leg Byes .......................................... | |
| How out ................................................. | | Bowling Average ................................... | |
| **Fielding** | | Analysis of Wickets Taken ................. | |
| Main Positions ..................................... | |     Bowled ............................................. | |
| ...................................... | |     Caught .............................................. | |
| Catches ................................................. | |     Caught & Bowled ........................... | |
| Run out ................................................. | |     L.B.W. ............................................... | |
| *Stumped ............................................... | |     Other ................................................. | |
| *Byes ...................................................... | | | |
| *If Keeping Wicket | | Total Number of Bowlers ................... | |

## NOTES

Weather and Effect on Game

Injuries

Other Useful Notes

Date ..............................20..... v. ........................................ C.C. Home/Away
League ................................ Division ............. Overs ............. Players ...............

## TEAM RESULT:

Won/Lost/Drawn by .................. Runs/by .................. Wickets .................. Points
Our Runs ............... Wickets ............... Their Runs ............... Wickets ...............

## PERSONAL RECORD

| Batting | Rating | Bowling | Rating |
|---|---|---|---|

**Batting** | Rating
Batting Order .................................... 
Runs .................................... 
Number of 6's .................................... 
Number of 4's .................................... 
Wicket Partnership .................................... 
    Name .................................... 
    Runs .................................... 
Number of Overs .................................... 
Number balls faced .................................... 
How out .................................... 

**Fielding**
Main Positions ....................................
....................................
Catches ....................................
Run out ....................................
*Stumped ....................................
*Byes ....................................
*If Keeping Wicket

**Bowling** | Rating
Number of Overs ....................................
Maiden Overs ....................................
Wickets ....................................
Runs ....................................
Extras ....................................
    No Balls ....................................
    Wides ....................................
    Byes ....................................
    Leg Byes ....................................
Bowling Average ....................................
Analysis of Wickets Taken ..................
    Bowled ....................................
    Caught ....................................
    Caught & Bowled ....................................
    L.B.W. ....................................
    Other ....................................

Total Number of Bowlers ....................

## NOTES

Weather and Effect on Game

Injuries

Other Useful Notes

Date ..................................20..... v. ........................................ C.C. Home/Away
League ................................. Division ............. Overs ............. Players ...............

## TEAM RESULT:

Won/Lost/Drawn by .................. Runs/by .................. Wickets .................. Points
Our Runs ............... Wickets ............... Their Runs ............... Wickets ...............

## PERSONAL RECORD

| **Batting** | Rating | **Bowling** | Rating |
|---|---|---|---|

Batting Order ...................................... | Number of Overs ......................................
Runs ...................................... | Maiden Overs ......................................
Number of 6's ...................................... | Wickets ......................................
Number of 4's ...................................... | Runs ......................................
Wicket Partnership ...................... | Extras ......................................
    Name ...................................... |     No Balls ......................................
    Runs ...................................... |     Wides ......................................
Number of Overs ...................................... |     Byes ......................................
Number balls faced ...................................... |     Leg Byes ......................................
How out ...................................... | Bowling Average ......................................

**Fielding** | Analysis of Wickets Taken ..................
Main Positions ...................................... |     Bowled ......................................
...................................... |     Caught ......................................
Catches ...................................... |     Caught & Bowled ......................................
Run out ...................................... |     L.B.W. ......................................
*Stumped ...................................... |     Other ......................................
*Byes ...................................... |
*If Keeping Wicket | Total Number of Bowlers ......................

## NOTES

Weather and Effect on Game

Injuries

Other Useful Notes

Date ..........................................20..... v. ........................................ C.C. Home/Away
League ................................ Division ............ Overs ............. Players ..............

## TEAM RESULT:

Won/Lost/Drawn by .................. Runs/by .................. Wickets ................. Points
Our Runs ............... Wickets ............... Their Runs ............... Wickets ...............

## PERSONAL RECORD

| Batting | Rating | Bowling | Rating |
|---|---|---|---|
| Batting Order ...................................... | | Number of Overs ............................. | |
| Runs ...................................................... | | Maiden Overs .................................. | |
| Number of 6's ..................................... | | Wickets ............................................. | |
| Number of 4's ..................................... | | Runs .................................................. | |
| Wicket Partnership ............................ | | Extras ................................................ | |
|     Name ............................................ | |     No Balls ..................................... | |
|     Runs .............................................. | |     Wides ......................................... | |
| Number of Overs ................................ | |     Byes ........................................... | |
| Number balls faced ............................ | |     Leg Byes .................................... | |
| How out ............................................... | | Bowling Average ............................. | |
| **Fielding** | | Analysis of Wickets Taken ............... | |
| Main Positions ..................................... | |     Bowled ....................................... | |
| ........................................ | |     Caught ........................................ | |
| Catches ............................................... | |     Caught & Bowled ....................... | |
| Run out ................................................ | |     L.B.W. ......................................... | |
| *Stumped ............................................ | |     Other .......................................... | |
| *Byes ................................................... | | | |
| *If Keeping Wicket | | Total Number of Bowlers ................... | |

## NOTES

Weather and Effect on Game

Injuries

Other Useful Notes

Date ........................................20..... v. ......................................... C.C. Home/Away
League ................................ Division ............. Overs ............. Players ...............

## TEAM RESULT:

Won/Lost/Drawn by .................. Runs/by .................. Wickets .................. Points
Our Runs ............... Wickets ............... Their Runs ............... Wickets ...............

## PERSONAL RECORD

| Batting | Rating | Bowling | Rating |
|---|---|---|---|
| Batting Order ............................................... | | Number of Overs ............................... | |
| Runs ............................................................... | | Maiden Overs ..................................... | |
| Number of 6's ............................................ | | Wickets ................................................. | |
| Number of 4's ............................................ | | Runs ...................................................... | |
| Wicket Partnership .................................... | | Extras ................................................... | |
|     Name ................................................... | |     No Balls ......................................... | |
|     Runs .................................................... | |     Wides ............................................. | |
| Number of Overs ....................................... | |     Byes ............................................... | |
| Number balls faced ................................... | |     Leg Byes ....................................... | |
| How out ...................................................... | | Bowling Average ............................... | |
| **Fielding** | | Analysis of Wickets Taken ............. | |
| Main Positions ........................................... | |     Bowled ........................................... | |
| ....................................... | |     Caught ........................................... | |
| Catches ....................................................... | |     Caught & Bowled ......................... | |
| Run out ...................................................... | |     L.B.W. ............................................ | |
| *Stumped ................................................... | |     Other .............................................. | |
| *Byes .......................................................... | | | |
| *If Keeping Wicket | | Total Number of Bowlers ............... | |

## NOTES

Weather and Effect on Game

Injuries

Other Useful Notes

Date ........................................20..... v. ........................................ C.C. Home/Away
League ............................ Division ............ Overs ............ Players ..............

---

## TEAM RESULT:

Won/Lost/Drawn by .................. Runs/by .................. Wickets .................. Points
Our Runs ............... Wickets ............... Their Runs ............... Wickets ...............

---

## PERSONAL RECORD

| Batting | Rating | Bowling | Rating |
|---|---|---|---|
| Batting Order ................................ | | Number of Overs ............................ | |
| Runs .................................................. | | Maiden Overs ................................. | |
| Number of 6's ................................. | | Wickets ............................................ | |
| Number of 4's ................................. | | Runs .................................................. | |
| Wicket Partnership ......................... | | Extras ................................................ | |
|     Name ........................................ | |     No Balls ................................. | |
|     Runs .......................................... | |     Wides ...................................... | |
| Number of Overs ............................. | |     Byes ......................................... | |
| Number balls faced ......................... | |     Leg Byes ................................. | |
| How out ............................................ | | Bowling Average ............................. | |
| **Fielding** | | Analysis of Wickets Taken .............. | |
| Main Positions ................................ | |     Bowled ................................... | |
| ..................................... | |     Caught .................................... | |
| Catches ............................................ | |     Caught & Bowled .................... | |
| Run out ............................................. | |     L.B.W. ..................................... | |
| *Stumped ........................................ | |     Other ....................................... | |
| *Byes ................................................ | | | |
| *If Keeping Wicket | | Total Number of Bowlers .................... | |

## NOTES

Weather and Effect on Game

Injuries

Other Useful Notes

Date ........................................20..... v. ........................................ C.C. Home/Away
League ................................. Division ............. Overs ............. Players ...............

## TEAM RESULT:

Won/Lost/Drawn by .................. Runs/by .................. Wickets .................. Points
Our Runs ............... Wickets ............... Their Runs ............... Wickets ...............

## PERSONAL RECORD

| Batting | Rating | Bowling | Rating |
|---|---|---|---|
| Batting Order ....................................... | | Number of Overs ........................... | |
| Runs ....................................................... | | Maiden Overs ................................. | |
| Number of 6's ..................................... | | Wickets ............................................. | |
| Number of 4's ..................................... | | Runs ................................................. | |
| Wicket Partnership ........................... | | Extras ............................................... | |
|     Name ............................................. | |     No Balls ..................................... | |
|     Runs ............................................... | |     Wides ......................................... | |
| Number of Overs ............................... | |     Byes ............................................. | |
| Number balls faced ......................... | |     Leg Byes ..................................... | |
| How out ............................................... | | Bowling Average ........................... | |
| **Fielding** | | Analysis of Wickets Taken ......... | |
| Main Positions ................................... | |     Bowled ....................................... | |
| ............................................................... | |     Caught ....................................... | |
| Catches ............................................... | |     Caught & Bowled ..................... | |
| Run out ............................................... | |     L.B.W. ......................................... | |
| *Stumped ........................................... | |     Other ........................................... | |
| *Byes ................................................... | | | |
| *If Keeping Wicket | | Total Number of Bowlers ............ | |

## NOTES

Weather and Effect on Game

Injuries

Other Useful Notes

Date ........................................20..... v. ........................................ C.C. Home/Away
League ................................ Division ............ Overs ............ Players ..............

## TEAM RESULT:

Won/Lost/Drawn by ................. Runs/by ................. Wickets ................. Points
Our Runs ............... Wickets ............... Their Runs ............... Wickets ...............

## PERSONAL RECORD

| Batting | Rating | Bowling | Rating |
|---|---|---|---|

Batting Order ...................................... | Number of Overs ..............................
Runs .................................................... | Maiden Overs ....................................
Number of 6's .................................... | Wickets ..............................................
Number of 4's .................................... | Runs ..................................................
Wicket Partnership ........................... | Extras ................................................
    Name ............................................ |     No Balls ....................................
    Runs ............................................. |     Wides .........................................
Number of Overs ............................... |     Byes ...........................................
Number balls faced .......................... |     Leg Byes ...................................
How out .............................................. | Bowling Average ..............................

**Fielding** | Analysis of Wickets Taken .................
Main Positions .................................. |     Bowled .......................................
.............................................................. |     Caught .......................................
Catches .............................................. |     Caught & Bowled .......................
Run out .............................................. |     L.B.W. ........................................
*Stumped ........................................... |     Other ..........................................
*Byes ..................................................
*If Keeping Wicket | Total Number of Bowlers .....................

## NOTES

Weather and Effect on Game

Injuries

Other Useful Notes

Date ........................................20..... v. ........................................ C.C. Home/Away
League ................................ Division ............. Overs ............. Players ...............

## TEAM RESULT:

Won/Lost/Drawn by .................. Runs/by .................. Wickets .................. Points
Our Runs ............... Wickets ...............  Their Runs ............... Wickets ...............

## PERSONAL RECORD

| Batting | Rating | Bowling | Rating |
|---|---|---|---|
| Batting Order ........................................ | | Number of Overs ........................... | |
| Runs ........................................................ | | Maiden Overs ................................. | |
| Number of 6's ........................................ | | Wickets ............................................ | |
| Number of 4's ........................................ | | Runs ................................................. | |
| Wicket Partnership ............................. | | Extras ............................................... | |
|     Name ................................................ | |     No Balls ....................................... | |
|     Runs ................................................. | |     Wides ........................................... | |
| Number of Overs ................................. | |     Byes .............................................. | |
| Number balls faced ............................ | |     Leg Byes ...................................... | |
| How out ................................................. | | Bowling Average ........................... | |
| **Fielding** | | Analysis of Wickets Taken ......... | |
| Main Positions ...................................... | |     Bowled ......................................... | |
|                     ......................................... | |     Caught .......................................... | |
| Catches .................................................. | |     Caught & Bowled ....................... | |
| Run out .................................................. | |     L.B.W. ........................................... | |
| *Stumped ............................................... | |     Other ............................................. | |
| *Byes ...................................................... | | | |
| *If Keeping Wicket | | Total Number of Bowlers ................. | |

## NOTES

Weather and Effect on Game

Injuries

Other Useful Notes

Date ........................20..... v. ........................ C.C. Home/Away
League ................................ Division ............. Overs ............ Players ..............

## TEAM RESULT:

Won/Lost/Drawn by .................. Runs/by .................. Wickets .................. Points
Our Runs ............... Wickets ............... Their Runs ............... Wickets ...............

## PERSONAL RECORD

| Batting | Rating | Bowling | Rating |
|---|---|---|---|
| Batting Order ........................ | | Number of Overs ........................ | |
| Runs ........................ | | Maiden Overs ........................ | |
| Number of 6's ........................ | | Wickets ........................ | |
| Number of 4's ........................ | | Runs ........................ | |
| Wicket Partnership ........................ | | Extras ........................ | |
|     Name ........................ | |     No Balls ........................ | |
|     Runs ........................ | |     Wides ........................ | |
| Number of Overs ........................ | |     Byes ........................ | |
| Number balls faced ........................ | |     Leg Byes ........................ | |
| How out ........................ | | Bowling Average ........................ | |
| **Fielding** | | Analysis of Wickets Taken ........ | |
| Main Positions ........................ | |     Bowled ........................ | |
| ........................ | |     Caught ........................ | |
| Catches ........................ | |     Caught & Bowled ........................ | |
| Run out ........................ | |     L.B.W. ........................ | |
| *Stumped ........................ | |     Other ........................ | |
| *Byes ........................ | | | |
| *If Keeping Wicket | | Total Number of Bowlers ............ | |

## NOTES

Weather and Effect on Game

Injuries

Other Useful Notes

Date ........................................20..... v. ........................................ C.C. Home/Away
League ................................ Division ............. Overs ............. Players ...............

## TEAM RESULT:

Won/Lost/Drawn by .................. Runs/by .................. Wickets .................. Points
Our Runs ............... Wickets ...............  Their Runs ............... Wickets ...............

## PERSONAL RECORD

| Batting | Rating | Bowling | Rating |
|---|---|---|---|
| Batting Order ........................... | ............... | Number of Overs ........................... | ............... |
| Runs ........................................... | ............... | Maiden Overs ........................... | ............... |
| Number of 6's ........................... | ............... | Wickets ........................................... | ............... |
| Number of 4's ........................... | ............... | Runs ........................................... | ............... |
| Wicket Partnership ........................... | ............... | Extras ........................................... | ............... |
|     Name ........................................... | ............... |     No Balls ........................... | ............... |
|     Runs ........................................... | ............... |     Wides ........................................... | ............... |
| Number of Overs ........................... | ............... |     Byes ........................................... | ............... |
| Number balls faced ........................... | ............... |     Leg Byes ........................... | ............... |
| How out ........................................... | ............... | Bowling Average ........................... | ............... |
| **Fielding** | | Analysis of Wickets Taken ........ | ............... |
| Main Positions ........................... | ............... |     Bowled ........................................... | ............... |
| ........................... | ............... |     Caught ........................................... | ............... |
| Catches ........................................... | ............... |     Caught & Bowled ........................... | ............... |
| Run out ........................................... | ............... |     L.B.W. ........................................... | ............... |
| *Stumped ........................................... | ............... |     Other ........................................... | ............... |
| *Byes ........................................... | ............... | | |
| *If Keeping Wicket | | Total Number of Bowlers ........ | ............... |

## NOTES

Weather and Effect on Game

Injuries

Other Useful Notes

Date ........................20..... v. ........................ C.C. Home/Away
League ................... Division ............ Overs ............ Players ...............

## TEAM RESULT:

Won/Lost/Drawn by ................. Runs/by ................. Wickets ................. Points
Our Runs ............... Wickets ............... Their Runs ............... Wickets ...............

## PERSONAL RECORD

| Batting | Rating | Bowling | Rating |
|---|---|---|---|
| Batting Order ........................ | | Number of Overs ........................ | |
| Runs ........................ | | Maiden Overs ........................ | |
| Number of 6's ........................ | | Wickets ........................ | |
| Number of 4's ........................ | | Runs ........................ | |
| Wicket Partnership ........................ | | Extras ........................ | |
|     Name ........................ | |     No Balls ........................ | |
|     Runs ........................ | |     Wides ........................ | |
| Number of Overs ........................ | |     Byes ........................ | |
| Number balls faced ........................ | |     Leg Byes ........................ | |
| How out ........................ | | Bowling Average ........................ | |
| **Fielding** | | Analysis of Wickets Taken ........................ | |
| Main Positions ........................ | |     Bowled ........................ | |
| ........................ | |     Caught ........................ | |
| Catches ........................ | |     Caught & Bowled ........................ | |
| Run out ........................ | |     L.B.W. ........................ | |
| *Stumped ........................ | |     Other ........................ | |
| *Byes ........................ | | | |
| *If Keeping Wicket | | Total Number of Bowlers ........................ | |

## NOTES

Weather and Effect on Game

Injuries

Other Useful Notes

Date ........................................20..... v. ........................................ C.C. Home/Away
League ................................ Division ............. Overs ............. Players ..............

---

## TEAM RESULT:

Won/Lost/Drawn by ................... Runs/by ................... Wickets ................... Points
Our Runs ............... Wickets ............... Their Runs ............... Wickets ...............

---

## PERSONAL RECORD

| Batting | Rating | Bowling | Rating |
|---|---|---|---|
| Batting Order .................................. | | Number of Overs ............................ | |
| Runs ................................................. | | Maiden Overs ................................. | |
| Number of 6's .................................. | | Wickets ............................................ | |
| Number of 4's .................................. | | Runs ................................................. | |
| Wicket Partnership ......................... | | Extras ............................................... | |
|     Name ..................................... | |     No Balls ....................................... | |
|     Runs ...................................... | |     Wides ........................................... | |
| Number of Overs ............................. | |     Byes .............................................. | |
| Number balls faced ......................... | |     Leg Byes ...................................... | |
| How out ............................................. | | Bowling Average ............................ | |
| **Fielding** | | Analysis of Wickets Taken ............ | |
| Main Positions ................................. | |     Bowled ......................................... | |
| .......................................... | |     Caught .......................................... | |
| Catches ............................................. | |     Caught & Bowled ........................ | |
| Run out ............................................. | |     L.B.W. .......................................... | |
| *Stumped ......................................... | |     Other ............................................. | |
| *Byes ................................................. | | | |
| *If Keeping Wicket | | Total Number of Bowlers ................ | |

## NOTES

Weather and Effect on Game

Injuries

Other Useful Notes

Date ........................................20..... v. ......................................... C.C. Home/Away
League ................................ Division ............. Overs ............. Players ...............

---

## TEAM RESULT:

Won/Lost/Drawn by .................. Runs/by .................. Wickets .................. Points
Our Runs ............... Wickets ............... Their Runs ............... Wickets ...............

---

## PERSONAL RECORD

| **Batting** | Rating | **Bowling** | Rating |
|---|---|---|---|

Batting Order ........................................  Number of Overs ...............................
Runs ......................................................  Maiden Overs ......................................
Number of 6's ......................................  Wickets ................................................
Number of 4's ......................................  Runs ....................................................
Wicket Partnership ............................  Extras ..................................................
    Name ..........................................      No Balls ......................................
    Runs ...........................................      Wides .........................................
Number of Overs ................................      Byes ............................................
Number balls faced ...........................      Leg Byes ....................................
How out ..............................................  Bowling Average ................................

**Fielding**  Analysis of Wickets Taken ..............
Main Positions ...................................      Bowled ........................................
..............................................................      Caught .........................................
Catches ...............................................      Caught & Bowled .......................
Run out ...............................................      L.B.W. .........................................
*Stumped ...........................................      Other ..........................................
*Byes ..................................................
*If Keeping Wicket  Total Number of Bowlers ..................

---

## NOTES

Weather and Effect on Game

Injuries

Other Useful Notes

Date ........................................20..... v. ........................................ C.C. Home/Away
League ................................. Division ............. Overs ............. Players ..............

## TEAM RESULT:

Won/Lost/Drawn by .................. Runs/by .................. Wickets .................. Points
Our Runs ............... Wickets ...............   Their Runs ............... Wickets ...............

## PERSONAL RECORD

| Batting | Rating | Bowling | Rating |
|---|---|---|---|

Batting Order ...................................   Number of Overs .................................
Runs ...................................................   Maiden Overs ......................................
Number of 6's ....................................   Wickets ................................................
Number of 4's ....................................   Runs ....................................................
Wicket Partnership ............................   Extras ..................................................
     Name ........................................        No Balls ........................................
     Runs .........................................        Wides ...........................................
Number of Overs ...............................        Byes .............................................
Number balls faced ...........................        Leg Byes ......................................
How out ..............................................   Bowling Average ................................

**Fielding**   Analysis of Wickets Taken ..................

Main Positions ...................................        Bowled ..........................................
     .............................................        Caught ..........................................
Catches ...............................................        Caught & Bowled .......................
Run out ...............................................        L.B.W. ...........................................
*Stumped ............................................        Other .............................................
*Byes ....................................................
*If Keeping Wicket   Total Number of Bowlers ....................

## NOTES

Weather and Effect on Game

Injuries

Other Useful Notes

Date ........................................20..... v. ........................................ C.C. Home/Away
League ................................ Division ............. Overs ............. Players ..............

---

## TEAM RESULT:

Won/Lost/Drawn by .................. Runs/by .................. Wickets .................. Points
Our Runs ............... Wickets ............... Their Runs ............... Wickets ...............

---

## PERSONAL RECORD

| Batting | Rating | Bowling | Rating |
|---|---|---|---|

**Batting** — Rating

Batting Order ...................................
Runs ..................................................
Number of 6's ...................................
Number of 4's ...................................
Wicket Partnership ............................
    Name ..........................................
    Runs ...........................................
Number of Overs ...............................
Number balls faced ...........................
How out .............................................

**Fielding**

Main Positions ..................................
.................................
Catches .............................................
Run out ..............................................
*Stumped ..........................................
*Byes .................................................
*If Keeping Wicket

**Bowling** — Rating

Number of Overs ...............................
Maiden Overs ...................................
Wickets .............................................
Runs ..................................................
Extras ................................................
    No Balls ......................................
    Wides ..........................................
    Byes ............................................
    Leg Byes .....................................
Bowling Average ...............................
Analysis of Wickets Taken ................
    Bowled .......................................
    Caught ........................................
    Caught & Bowled .......................
    L.B.W. .........................................
    Other ..........................................

Total Number of Bowlers ..................

---

## NOTES

Weather and Effect on Game

Injuries

Other Useful Notes

Date ........................................20..... v. ........................................ C.C. Home/Away
League ................................ Division ............ Overs ............ Players ..............

## TEAM RESULT:

Won/Lost/Drawn by ................. Runs/by ................. Wickets ................. Points
Our Runs ............... Wickets ...............   Their Runs ............... Wickets ...............

## PERSONAL RECORD

| Batting | Rating | Bowling | Rating |
|---|---|---|---|
| Batting Order ........................ | | Number of Overs ..................... | |
| Runs ..................................... | | Maiden Overs ......................... | |
| Number of 6's ........................ | | Wickets .................................. | |
| Number of 4's ........................ | | Runs ...................................... | |
| Wicket Partnership .............. | | Extras .................................... | |
|     Name ............................... | |     No Balls ........................... | |
|     Runs ................................ | |     Wides ............................... | |
| Number of Overs .................. | |     Byes ................................. | |
| Number balls faced ............. | |     Leg Byes .......................... | |
| How out ................................ | | Bowling Average ..................... | |
| **Fielding** | | Analysis of Wickets Taken ..... | |
| Main Positions ...................... | |     Bowled ............................. | |
| ............................... | |     Caught .............................. | |
| Catches ................................. | |     Caught & Bowled ............. | |
| Run out ................................. | |     L.B.W. ............................... | |
| *Stumped .............................. | |     Other ................................. | |
| *Byes .................................... | | | |
| *If Keeping Wicket | | Total Number of Bowlers ....... | |

## NOTES

Weather and Effect on Game

Injuries

Other Useful Notes

Date ........................................20..... v. ........................................ C.C. Home/Away
League ................................ Division ............. Overs ............. Players ..............

---

## TEAM RESULT:

Won/Lost/Drawn by .................. Runs/by .................. Wickets .................. Points
Our Runs ............... Wickets ................ Their Runs ............... Wickets ...............

---

## PERSONAL RECORD

| Batting | Rating | Bowling | Rating |
|---|---|---|---|

Batting Order ........................................ | Number of Overs ...............................
Runs ..................................................... | Maiden Overs ......................................
Number of 6's ....................................... | Wickets ................................................
Number of 4's ....................................... | Runs .....................................................
Wicket Partnership ............................. | Extras ..................................................
    Name ........................................... |     No Balls ......................................
    Runs ............................................ |     Wides ..........................................
Number of Overs ................................ |     Byes ............................................
Number balls faced ............................ |     Leg Byes ....................................
How out .............................................. | Bowling Average ...............................
**Fielding** | Analysis of Wickets Taken .................
Main Positions ................................... |     Bowled .......................................
                                        ........................ |     Caught .......................................
Catches ............................................... |     Caught & Bowled .......................
Run out ............................................... |     L.B.W. ..........................................
*Stumped ............................................ |     Other ..........................................
*Byes .................................................. |
*If Keeping Wicket | Total Number of Bowlers ..................

---

## NOTES

Weather and Effect on Game

Injuries

Other Useful Notes

Date .............................20..... v. ........................................ C.C. Home/Away
League ............................... Division ............. Overs ............ Players ..............

## TEAM RESULT:

Won/Lost/Drawn by ................. Runs/by ................. Wickets ................. Points
Our Runs ............... Wickets ................ Their Runs ............... Wickets ..............

## PERSONAL RECORD

| Batting | Rating | Bowling | Rating |
|---|---|---|---|

Batting Order ........................................ | Number of Overs ..............................
Runs ....................................................... | Maiden Overs ......................................
Number of 6's ...................................... | Wickets .................................................
Number of 4's ...................................... | Runs .....................................................
Wicket Partnership ............................ | Extras ...................................................
    Name ............................................... |     No Balls ..........................................
    Runs ................................................ |     Wides ..............................................
Number of Overs ................................ |     Byes .................................................
Number balls faced ........................... |     Leg Byes .........................................
How out ................................................ | Bowling Average ................................

**Fielding** | Analysis of Wickets Taken ..............
Main Positions .................................... |     Bowled ............................................
    ................................................................ |     Caught ............................................
Catches ................................................ |     Caught & Bowled .......................
Run out ................................................ |     L.B.W. .............................................
*Stumped ............................................. |     Other ...............................................
*Byes .....................................................
*If Keeping Wicket | Total Number of Bowlers ................

## NOTES

Weather and Effect on Game

Injuries

Other Useful Notes

Date .........................................20..... v. ......................................... C.C. Home/Away
League ................................ Division ............ Overs ............ Players ..............

## TEAM RESULT:

Won/Lost/Drawn by .................. Runs/by .................. Wickets .................. Points
Our Runs ............... Wickets ................ Their Runs ............... Wickets ...............

## PERSONAL RECORD

| **Batting** | Rating | **Bowling** | Rating |
|---|---|---|---|
| Batting Order ..................................... | | Number of Overs ................................ | |
| Runs ................................................. | | Maiden Overs .................................... | |
| Number of 6's .................................... | | Wickets .............................................. | |
| Number of 4's .................................... | | Runs ................................................... | |
| Wicket Partnership ............................ | | Extras ................................................. | |
|     Name ................................... | |     No Balls ....................................... | |
|     Runs .................................... | |     Wides ........................................... | |
| Number of Overs ................................ | |     Byes ............................................. | |
| Number balls faced ........................... | |     Leg Byes ...................................... | |
| How out ............................................. | | Bowling Average ................................ | |
| **Fielding** | | Analysis of Wickets Taken ................ | |
| Main Positions .................................. | |     Bowled ......................................... | |
| ........................................ | |     Caught .......................................... | |
| Catches ............................................. | |     Caught & Bowled ......................... | |
| Run out ............................................. | |     L.B.W. ........................................... | |
| *Stumped .......................................... | |     Other ............................................ | |
| *Byes ................................................. | | | |
| *If Keeping Wicket | | Total Number of Bowlers .................... | |

## NOTES

Weather and Effect on Game

Injuries

Other Useful Notes

Date .........................20..... v. ......................................... C.C. Home/Away
League ............................... Division ............ Overs ............. Players ...............

## TEAM RESULT:

Won/Lost/Drawn by .................. Runs/by ................. Wickets ................. Points
Our Runs ............... Wickets ...............  Their Runs ............... Wickets ...............

## PERSONAL RECORD

| Batting | Rating | Bowling | Rating |
|---|---|---|---|

Batting Order ....................................... | Number of Overs ............................
Runs ..................................................... | Maiden Overs ..................................
Number of 6's ...................................... | Wickets ............................................
Number of 4's ...................................... | Runs ..................................................
Wicket Partnership ............................ | Extras ...............................................
    Name ............................................ |     No Balls ......................................
    Runs ............................................. |     Wides ..........................................
Number of Overs ................................ |     Byes .............................................
Number balls faced ........................... |     Leg Byes ......................................
How out ............................................... | Bowling Average .............................

**Fielding** | Analysis of Wickets Taken .............
Main Positions .................................... |     Bowled .........................................
........................................ |     Caught .........................................
Catches ............................................... |     Caught & Bowled ........................
Run out ................................................ |     L.B.W. ..........................................
*Stumped ............................................ |     Other ............................................
*Byes ....................................................
*If Keeping Wicket | Total Number of Bowlers ...............

## NOTES

Weather and Effect on Game

Injuries

Other Useful Notes

Date ........................................20..... v. ........................................ C.C. Home/Away
League ................................ Division ............ Overs ............ Players ..............

## TEAM RESULT:

Won/Lost/Drawn by .................. Runs/by .................. Wickets .................. Points
Our Runs ............... Wickets ...............    Their Runs ............... Wickets ...............

## PERSONAL RECORD

| Batting | Rating | Bowling | Rating |
|---|---|---|---|
| Batting Order ........................................ | | Number of Overs ............................ | |
| Runs ................................................... | | Maiden Overs ................................. | |
| Number of 6's ..................................... | | Wickets ............................................ | |
| Number of 4's ..................................... | | Runs ................................................ | |
| Wicket Partnership ............................ | | Extras .............................................. | |
|     Name ........................................... | |     No Balls ..................................... | |
|     Runs ............................................ | |     Wides ......................................... | |
| Number of Overs ................................ | |     Byes ........................................... | |
| Number balls faced ............................ | |     Leg Byes .................................... | |
| How out .............................................. | | Bowling Average ............................. | |
| **Fielding** | | Analysis of Wickets Taken ............ | |
| Main Positions .................................... | |     Bowled ....................................... | |
|     ........................................................ | |     Caught ........................................ | |
| Catches ............................................... | |     Caught & Bowled ....................... | |
| Run out ............................................... | |     L.B.W. ......................................... | |
| *Stumped ........................................... | |     Other .......................................... | |
| *Byes .................................................. | | | |
| *If Keeping Wicket | | Total Number of Bowlers ................ | |

## NOTES

Weather and Effect on Game

Injuries

Other Useful Notes

Date .................................20..... v. ....................................... C.C. Home/Away
League ................................ Division ............. Overs ............ Players ...............

## TEAM RESULT:

Won/Lost/Drawn by .................. Runs/by ................. Wickets ................. Points
Our Runs .............. Wickets ............... Their Runs ............... Wickets ..............

## PERSONAL RECORD

| Batting | Rating | Bowling | Rating |
|---|---|---|---|
| Batting Order ......................................... | | Number of Overs ............................. | |
| Runs ........................................................ | | Maiden Overs ................................... | |
| Number of 6's ....................................... | | Wickets ............................................... | |
| Number of 4's ....................................... | | Runs .................................................... | |
| Wicket Partnership ............................ | | Extras .................................................. | |
| Name .......................................... | | No Balls ..................................... | |
| Runs ............................................ | | Wides .......................................... | |
| Number of Overs ................................. | | Byes ............................................ | |
| Number balls faced ............................ | | Leg Byes .................................... | |
| How out ................................................. | | Bowling Average ............................. | |
| **Fielding** | | Analysis of Wickets Taken ............ | |
| Main Positions .................................... | | Bowled ....................................... | |
| ................................. | | Caught ....................................... | |
| Catches .................................................. | | Caught & Bowled ..................... | |
| Run out .................................................. | | L.B.W. ......................................... | |
| *Stumped ............................................... | | Other .......................................... | |
| *Byes ...................................................... | | | |
| *If Keeping Wicket | | Total Number of Bowlers .................... | |

## NOTES

Weather and Effect on Game

Injuries

Other Useful Notes

Date .................................20..... v. ....................................... C.C. Home/Away
League ................................ Division ............. Overs ............. Players ..............

## TEAM RESULT:

Won/Lost/Drawn by .................. Runs/by .................. Wickets .................. Points
Our Runs ............... Wickets ............... Their Runs ............... Wickets ...............

## PERSONAL RECORD

| Batting | Rating | Bowling | Rating |
|---|---|---|---|
| Batting Order ..................................... | | Number of Overs .................................. | |
| Runs ..................................................... | | Maiden Overs ....................................... | |
| Number of 6's ...................................... | | Wickets ................................................. | |
| Number of 4's ...................................... | | Runs ..................................................... | |
| Wicket Partnership ............................. | | Extras ................................................... | |
|     Name ............................................ | |     No Balls ...................................... | |
|     Runs ............................................. | |     Wides ........................................... | |
| Number of Overs ................................ | |     Byes .............................................. | |
| Number balls faced ............................ | |     Leg Byes ...................................... | |
| How out ............................................... | | Bowling Average .................................. | |
| **Fielding** | | Analysis of Wickets Taken .................. | |
| Main Positions .................................... | |     Bowled ......................................... | |
| ................................... | |     Caught .......................................... | |
| Catches ................................................ | |     Caught & Bowled ........................ | |
| Run out ................................................ | |     L.B.W. ........................................... | |
| *Stumped ............................................. | |     Other ............................................. | |
| *Byes .................................................... | | | |
| *If Keeping Wicket | | Total Number of Bowlers ..................... | |

## NOTES

Weather and Effect on Game

Injuries

Other Useful Notes

Date ........................................20..... v. ...................................... C.C. Home/Away
League ................................ Division ............. Overs ............. Players ...............

## TEAM RESULT:

Won/Lost/Drawn by .................. Runs/by .................. Wickets .................. Points
Our Runs ............... Wickets ................   Their Runs ............... Wickets ...............

## PERSONAL RECORD

| Batting | Rating | Bowling | Rating |
|---|---|---|---|

**Batting**

Batting Order ........................................

Runs .......................................................

Number of 6's ......................................

Number of 4's ......................................

Wicket Partnership ............................

    Name ................................................

    Runs .................................................

Number of Overs ................................

Number balls faced ...........................

How out ................................................

**Fielding**

Main Positions ....................................

........................................

Catches ................................................

Run out ................................................

*Stumped ............................................

*Byes ....................................................

*If Keeping Wicket

**Bowling**

Number of Overs ................................

Maiden Overs .....................................

Wickets ................................................

Runs .....................................................

Extras ...................................................

    No Balls ...........................................

    Wides ...............................................

    Byes ..................................................

    Leg Byes ..........................................

Bowling Average ................................

Analysis of Wickets Taken ..................

    Bowled .............................................

    Caught ..............................................

    Caught & Bowled ..........................

    L.B.W. ...............................................

    Other .................................................

Total Number of Bowlers ....................

## NOTES

Weather and Effect on Game

Injuries

Other Useful Notes

Date ..................................20..... v. ...................................... C.C. Home/Away
League ................................. Division ............ Overs ............. Players ..............

## TEAM RESULT:

Won/Lost/Drawn by .................. Runs/by .................. Wickets .................. Points
Our Runs ................ Wickets ............... Their Runs ............... Wickets ...............

## PERSONAL RECORD

| **Batting** | Rating | **Bowling** | Rating |
|---|---|---|---|

Batting Order .....................................    Number of Overs ..............................
Runs ....................................................    Maiden Overs ....................................
Number of 6's ...................................    Wickets ..............................................
Number of 4's ...................................    Runs ..................................................
Wicket Partnership ..........................    Extras ................................................
    Name ..........................................        No Balls .......................................
    Runs ...........................................        Wides ...........................................
Number of Overs .............................        Byes ..............................................
Number balls faced ..........................        Leg Byes .......................................
How out ............................................    Bowling Average ..............................

**Fielding**                                             Analysis of Wickets Taken ..................

Main Positions .................................        Bowled ..........................................
    ....................................        Caught ..........................................
Catches .............................................        Caught & Bowled .........................
Run out .............................................        L.B.W. ...........................................
*Stumped .........................................        Other .............................................
*Byes .................................................
*If Keeping Wicket                                  Total Number of Bowlers ....................

## NOTES

Weather and Effect on Game

Injuries

Other Useful Notes

Date ..................................20..... v. ........................................ C.C. Home/Away
League ................................. Division ............. Overs ............. Players ...............

## TEAM RESULT:

Won/Lost/Drawn by ................... Runs/by .................. Wickets .................. Points
Our Runs ............... Wickets ............... Their Runs ............... Wickets ...............

## PERSONAL RECORD

| Batting | Rating | Bowling | Rating |
|---|---|---|---|
| Batting Order ................................. ............... | | Number of Overs ................................ ............... | |
| Runs ................................................ ............... | | Maiden Overs ................................... ............... | |
| Number of 6's ................................ ............... | | Wickets ........................................... ............... | |
| Number of 4's ................................ ............... | | Runs ................................................ ............... | |
| Wicket Partnership ........................ ............... | | Extras .............................................. ............... | |
|     Name ........................................ ............... | |     No Balls ..................................... ............... | |
|     Runs ......................................... ............... | |     Wides ........................................ ............... | |
| Number of Overs ........................... ............... | |     Byes .......................................... ............... | |
| Number balls faced ....................... ............... | |     Leg Byes ................................... ............... | |
| How out ........................................... ............... | | Bowling Average ............................ ............... | |
| **Fielding** | | Analysis of Wickets Taken ........... ............... | |
| Main Positions ............................... ............... | |     Bowled ...................................... ............... | |
| ............................................................ ............... | |     Caught ....................................... ............... | |
| Catches ........................................... ............... | |     Caught & Bowled ..................... ............... | |
| Run out ........................................... ............... | |     L.B.W. ....................................... ............... | |
| *Stumped ....................................... ............... | |     Other ......................................... ............... | |
| *Byes ............................................... ............... | | | |
| *If Keeping Wicket | | Total Number of Bowlers ............. ............... | |

## NOTES

Weather and Effect on Game

Injuries

Other Useful Notes

Date ........................................20..... v. ......................................... C.C. Home/Away
League .................................. Division ............. Overs ............. Players ..............

---

## TEAM RESULT:

Won/Lost/Drawn by .................. Runs/by .................. Wickets .................. Points
Our Runs ................ Wickets ................ Their Runs ................ Wickets ................

---

## PERSONAL RECORD

| Batting | Rating | Bowling | Rating |
|---|---|---|---|
| Batting Order ..................................... | | Number of Overs ..................... | |
| Runs ..................................................... | | Maiden Overs ........................... | |
| Number of 6's ................................... | | Wickets ....................................... | |
| Number of 4's ................................... | | Runs ............................................ | |
| Wicket Partnership ........................... | | Extras .......................................... | |
|     Name ............................................ | |     No Balls ................................... | |
|     Runs ............................................. | |     Wides ....................................... | |
| Number of Overs ............................. | |     Byes ......................................... | |
| Number balls faced ......................... | |     Leg Byes ................................. | |
| How out ............................................. | | Bowling Average ..................... | |
| **Fielding** | | Analysis of Wickets Taken ..... | |
| Main Positions ................................. | |     Bowled ..................................... | |
|     ............................................................. | |     Caught ...................................... | |
| Catches .............................................. | |     Caught & Bowled ................... | |
| Run out ............................................... | |     L.B.W. ....................................... | |
| *Stumped .......................................... | |     Other ......................................... | |
| *Byes ................................................... | | | |
| *If Keeping Wicket | | Total Number of Bowlers ..... | |

## NOTES

Weather and Effect on Game

Injuries

Other Useful Notes

Date .................................20..... v. ....................................... C.C. Home/Away
League ................................ Division ............. Overs ............. Players ...............

---

## TEAM RESULT:

Won/Lost/Drawn by .................. Runs/by .................. Wickets ................. Points
Our Runs ............... Wickets ............... Their Runs ............... Wickets ...............

---

## PERSONAL RECORD

| Batting | Rating | Bowling | Rating |
|---|---|---|---|
| Batting Order ........................................... | | Number of Overs ............................ | |
| Runs ............................................................. | | Maiden Overs ................................... | |
| Number of 6's ........................................... | | Wickets ............................................... | |
| Number of 4's ........................................... | | Runs ..................................................... | |
| Wicket Partnership ........................... | | Extras .................................................. | |
|     Name .................................................... | |     No Balls ........................................... | |
|     Runs ..................................................... | |     Wides ................................................ | |
| Number of Overs ................................... | |     Byes .................................................... | |
| Number balls faced ............................. | |     Leg Byes ........................................... | |
| How out ...................................................... | | Bowling Average ............................... | |
| **Fielding** | | Analysis of Wickets Taken .................. | |
| Main Positions ........................................ | |     Bowled .............................................. | |
|                      ................................... | |     Caught ............................................... | |
| Catches ....................................................... | |     Caught & Bowled ........................... | |
| Run out ....................................................... | |     L.B.W. ................................................ | |
| *Stumped .................................................... | |     Other ................................................... | |
| *Byes ............................................................. | | | |
| *If Keeping Wicket | | Total Number of Bowlers ................... | |

---

## NOTES

Weather and Effect on Game

Injuries

Other Useful Notes

Date ........................................20..... v. ........................................ C.C. Home/Away
League ................................ Division ............ Overs ............ Players ...............

## TEAM RESULT:

Won/Lost/Drawn by ................. Runs/by ................. Wickets ................. Points
Our Runs ............... Wickets ...............  Their Runs ............... Wickets ...............

## PERSONAL RECORD

| Batting | Rating | Bowling | Rating |
|---|---|---|---|
| Batting Order ....................................... | | Number of Overs ....................................... | |
| Runs ....................................... | | Maiden Overs ....................................... | |
| Number of 6's ....................................... | | Wickets ....................................... | |
| Number of 4's ....................................... | | Runs ....................................... | |
| Wicket Partnership ........................... | | Extras ....................................... | |
|     Name ....................................... | |     No Balls ....................................... | |
|     Runs ....................................... | |     Wides ....................................... | |
| Number of Overs ....................................... | |     Byes ....................................... | |
| Number balls faced ........................... | |     Leg Byes ....................................... | |
| How out ....................................... | | Bowling Average ....................................... | |
| **Fielding** | | Analysis of Wickets Taken ................. | |
| Main Positions ....................................... | |     Bowled ....................................... | |
| ....................................... | |     Caught ....................................... | |
| Catches ....................................... | |     Caught & Bowled ....................... | |
| Run out ....................................... | |     L.B.W. ....................................... | |
| *Stumped ....................................... | |     Other ....................................... | |
| *Byes ....................................... | | | |
| *If Keeping Wicket | | Total Number of Bowlers ................... | |

## NOTES

Weather and Effect on Game

Injuries

Other Useful Notes

Date ..........................................20..... v. ........................................ C.C. Home/Away
League ................................. Division ............. Overs ............. Players ..............

## TEAM RESULT:

Won/Lost/Drawn by .................. Runs/by .................. Wickets .................. Points
Our Runs ............... Wickets ............... Their Runs ............... Wickets ...............

## PERSONAL RECORD

| Batting | Rating | Bowling | Rating |
|---|---|---|---|
| Batting Order ................................... | | Number of Overs ................... | |
| Runs .................................................. | | Maiden Overs ......................... | |
| Number of 6's ................................. | | Wickets ................................... | |
| Number of 4's ................................. | | Runs ........................................ | |
| Wicket Partnership .......................... | | Extras ...................................... | |
|     Name ............................................ | |     No Balls ................................ | |
|     Runs .............................................. | |     Wides .................................... | |
| Number of Overs ............................. | |     Byes ....................................... | |
| Number balls faced ......................... | |     Leg Byes ............................... | |
| How out ........................................... | | Bowling Average ................... | |
| **Fielding** | | Analysis of Wickets Taken ................... | |
| Main Positions ................................ | |     Bowled .................................. | |
|     ............................................. | |     Caught .................................. | |
| Catches ............................................ | |     Caught & Bowled ................. | |
| Run out ............................................ | |     L.B.W. ................................... | |
| *Stumped ......................................... | |     Other ..................................... | |
| *Byes ............................................... | | | |
| *If Keeping Wicket | | Total Number of Bowlers ................... | |

## NOTES

Weather and Effect on Game

Injuries

Other Useful Notes

Date ........................................20..... v. ........................................ C.C. Home/Away
League ................................ Division ............. Overs ............. Players ..............

## TEAM RESULT:

Won/Lost/Drawn by .................. Runs/by .................. Wickets .................. Points
Our Runs ................ Wickets ................ Their Runs ................ Wickets ................

## PERSONAL RECORD

| Batting | Rating | Bowling | Rating |
|---|---|---|---|
| Batting Order ..................................... | | Number of Overs ..................................... | |
| Runs ..................................... | | Maiden Overs ..................................... | |
| Number of 6's ..................................... | | Wickets ..................................... | |
| Number of 4's ..................................... | | Runs ..................................... | |
| Wicket Partnership ..................................... | | Extras ..................................... | |
|     Name ..................................... | |     No Balls ..................................... | |
|     Runs ..................................... | |     Wides ..................................... | |
| Number of Overs ..................................... | |     Byes ..................................... | |
| Number balls faced ..................................... | |     Leg Byes ..................................... | |
| How out ..................................... | | Bowling Average ..................................... | |
| **Fielding** | | Analysis of Wickets Taken .................. | |
| Main Positions ..................................... | |     Bowled ..................................... | |
| ..................................... | |     Caught ..................................... | |
| Catches ..................................... | |     Caught & Bowled ..................................... | |
| Run out ..................................... | |     L.B.W. ..................................... | |
| *Stumped ..................................... | |     Other ..................................... | |
| *Byes ..................................... | | | |
| *If Keeping Wicket | | Total Number of Bowlers ..................... | |

## NOTES

Weather and Effect on Game

Injuries

Other Useful Notes

Date ........................................20..... v. ......................................... C.C. Home/Away
League ................................. Division ............. Overs ............. Players ..............

## TEAM RESULT:

Won/Lost/Drawn by .................. Runs/by .................. Wickets .................. Points
Our Runs ................ Wickets ................ Their Runs ................ Wickets ................

## PERSONAL RECORD

| Batting | Rating | Bowling | Rating |
|---|---|---|---|
| Batting Order ..................................... | | Number of Overs ..................................... | |
| Runs ..................................... | | Maiden Overs ..................................... | |
| Number of 6's ..................................... | | Wickets ..................................... | |
| Number of 4's ..................................... | | Runs ..................................... | |
| Wicket Partnership ..................................... | | Extras ..................................... | |
|     Name ..................................... | |     No Balls ..................................... | |
|     Runs ..................................... | |     Wides ..................................... | |
| Number of Overs ..................................... | |     Byes ..................................... | |
| Number balls faced ..................................... | |     Leg Byes ..................................... | |
| How out ..................................... | | Bowling Average ..................................... | |
| **Fielding** | | Analysis of Wickets Taken ..................................... | |
| Main Positions ..................................... | |     Bowled ..................................... | |
| ..................................... | |     Caught ..................................... | |
| Catches ..................................... | |     Caught & Bowled ..................................... | |
| Run out ..................................... | |     L.B.W. ..................................... | |
| *Stumped ..................................... | |     Other ..................................... | |
| *Byes ..................................... | | | |
| *If Keeping Wicket | | Total Number of Bowlers ..................... | |

## NOTES

Weather and Effect on Game

Injuries

Other Useful Notes

Date .................................20..... v. ...................................... C.C. Home/Away
League ................................. Division ............. Overs ............. Players ..............

## TEAM RESULT:

Won/Lost/Drawn by .................. Runs/by .................. Wickets .................. Points
Our Runs ............... Wickets ............... Their Runs ............... Wickets ...............

## PERSONAL RECORD

| **Batting** | Rating | **Bowling** | Rating |
|---|---|---|---|
| Batting Order ..................................... | | Number of Overs ................................ | |
| Runs ..................................................... | | Maiden Overs ..................................... | |
| Number of 6's ..................................... | | Wickets ................................................ | |
| Number of 4's ..................................... | | Runs ..................................................... | |
| Wicket Partnership ............................ | | Extras ................................................... | |
|     Name ............................................. | |     No Balls ........................................ | |
|     Runs .............................................. | |     Wides ............................................ | |
| Number of Overs ................................ | |     Byes .............................................. | |
| Number balls faced ........................... | |     Leg Byes ...................................... | |
| How out ............................................... | | Bowling Average ............................... | |
| **Fielding** | | Analysis of Wickets Taken ................. | |
| Main Positions .................................... | |     Bowled ......................................... | |
| ................................... | |     Caught .......................................... | |
| Catches ................................................ | |     Caught & Bowled ........................ | |
| Run out ................................................ | |     L.B.W. ........................................... | |
| *Stumped ............................................. | |     Other ............................................. | |
| *Byes ..................................................... | | | |
| *If Keeping Wicket | | Total Number of Bowlers ..................... | |

## NOTES

Weather and Effect on Game

Injuries

Other Useful Notes

Date ..............................20..... v. ........................................ C.C. Home/Away
League ................................. Division ............. Overs ............. Players ..............

## TEAM RESULT:

Won/Lost/Drawn by .................. Runs/by .................. Wickets .................. Points
Our Runs ................ Wickets ................ Their Runs ................ Wickets ................

## PERSONAL RECORD

| Batting | Rating | Bowling | Rating |
|---|---|---|---|
| Batting Order ........................ | | Number of Overs ........................ | |
| Runs .................................... | | Maiden Overs ............................ | |
| Number of 6's ....................... | | Wickets .................................... | |
| Number of 4's ....................... | | Runs ........................................ | |
| Wicket Partnership ............... | | Extras ...................................... | |
|     Name ............................ | |     No Balls ............................ | |
|     Runs ............................. | |     Wides ................................ | |
| Number of Overs .................. | |     Byes .................................. | |
| Number balls faced .............. | |     Leg Byes .......................... | |
| How out ................................ | | Bowling Average ...................... | |
| **Fielding** | | Analysis of Wickets Taken ...... | |
| Main Positions ...................... | |     Bowled ............................. | |
| ........................................... | |     Caught .............................. | |
| Catches ................................ | |     Caught & Bowled .............. | |
| Run out ................................. | |     L.B.W. ................................ | |
| *Stumped ............................. | |     Other ................................. | |
| *Byes .................................... | | | |
| *If Keeping Wicket | | Total Number of Bowlers ............. | |

## NOTES

Weather and Effect on Game

Injuries

Other Useful Notes

Date ..............................20..... v. ........................................ C.C. Home/Away
League ................................ Division ............. Overs ............. Players ..............

## TEAM RESULT:

Won/Lost/Drawn by ................. Runs/by ................. Wickets ................. Points
Our Runs .............. Wickets ............... Their Runs ............... Wickets ..............

## PERSONAL RECORD

| **Batting** | Rating | **Bowling** | Rating |
|---|---|---|---|

**Batting** | Rating
Batting Order ...........................................
Runs ........................................................
Number of 6's ..........................................
Number of 4's ..........................................
Wicket Partnership ..........................
    Name ............................................
    Runs .............................................
Number of Overs ....................................
Number balls faced ...........................
How out ..................................................

**Fielding**
Main Positions ......................................
..............................................
Catches ..................................................
Run out ..................................................
*Stumped ................................................
*Byes .......................................................
*If Keeping Wicket

**Bowling** | Rating
Number of Overs ...................................
Maiden Overs ........................................
Wickets ...................................................
Runs ........................................................
Extras .....................................................
    No Balls ........................................
    Wides ............................................
    Byes ..............................................
    Leg Byes .......................................
Bowling Average ...................................
Analysis of Wickets Taken ..................
    Bowled ..........................................
    Caught ..........................................
    Caught & Bowled ........................
    L.B.W. ...........................................
    Other .............................................

Total Number of Bowlers ....................

## NOTES

Weather and Effect on Game

Injuries

Other Useful Notes

Date ............................................. 20..... v. ......................................... C.C. Home/Away
League ................................ Division ............. Overs ............. Players ...............

## TEAM RESULT:

Won/Lost/Drawn by .................. Runs/by .................. Wickets .................. Points
Our Runs ............... Wickets ............... Their Runs ............... Wickets ...............

## PERSONAL RECORD

| Batting | Rating | Bowling | Rating |
|---|---|---|---|

Batting Order ......................................... | Number of Overs .........................................
Runs ......................................... | Maiden Overs .........................................
Number of 6's ......................................... | Wickets .........................................
Number of 4's ......................................... | Runs .........................................
Wicket Partnership ............................. | Extras .........................................
    Name ......................................... |     No Balls .........................................
    Runs ......................................... |     Wides .........................................
Number of Overs ......................................... |     Byes .........................................
Number balls faced ......................................... |     Leg Byes .........................................
How out ......................................... | Bowling Average .........................................

**Fielding** | Analysis of Wickets Taken ..................

Main Positions ......................................... |     Bowled .........................................
......................................... |     Caught .........................................
Catches ......................................... |     Caught & Bowled .........................................
Run out ......................................... |     L.B.W. .........................................
*Stumped ......................................... |     Other .........................................
*Byes .........................................
*If Keeping Wicket | Total Number of Bowlers .....................

## NOTES

Weather and Effect on Game

Injuries

Other Useful Notes

Date ........................................20..... v. ........................................ C.C. Home/Away
League ................................ Division ............ Overs ............ Players ..............

## TEAM RESULT:

Won/Lost/Drawn by .................. Runs/by .................. Wickets .................. Points
Our Runs ............... Wickets ............... Their Runs ............... Wickets ...............

## PERSONAL RECORD

| Batting | Rating | Bowling | Rating |
|---|---|---|---|

**Batting**

Batting Order ........................................
Runs ........................................
Number of 6's ........................................
Number of 4's ........................................
Wicket Partnership ........................................
    Name ........................................
    Runs ........................................
Number of Overs ........................................
Number balls faced ........................................
How out ........................................

**Fielding**

Main Positions ........................................
........................................
Catches ........................................
Run out ........................................
*Stumped ........................................
*Byes ........................................
*If Keeping Wicket

**Bowling**

Number of Overs ........................................
Maiden Overs ........................................
Wickets ........................................
Runs ........................................
Extras ........................................
    No Balls ........................................
    Wides ........................................
    Byes ........................................
    Leg Byes ........................................
Bowling Average ........................................
Analysis of Wickets Taken ..................
    Bowled ........................................
    Caught ........................................
    Caught & Bowled ........................
    L.B.W. ........................................
    Other ........................................

Total Number of Bowlers ..................

## NOTES

Weather and Effect on Game

Injuries

Other Useful Notes

Date ........................................20..... v. ........................................ C.C. Home/Away
League ................................. Division ............. Overs ............. Players .............

## TEAM RESULT:

Won/Lost/Drawn by .................. Runs/by .................. Wickets .................. Points
Our Runs ............... Wickets ............... Their Runs ............... Wickets ...............

## PERSONAL RECORD

| Batting | Rating | Bowling | Rating |
|---|---|---|---|
| Batting Order ........................ | | Number of Overs ........................ | |
| Runs ........................ | | Maiden Overs ........................ | |
| Number of 6's ........................ | | Wickets ........................ | |
| Number of 4's ........................ | | Runs ........................ | |
| Wicket Partnership ........................ | | Extras ........................ | |
|     Name ........................ | |     No Balls ........................ | |
|     Runs ........................ | |     Wides ........................ | |
| Number of Overs ........................ | |     Byes ........................ | |
| Number balls faced ........................ | |     Leg Byes ........................ | |
| How out ........................ | | Bowling Average ........................ | |
| **Fielding** | | Analysis of Wickets Taken ........ | |
| Main Positions ........................ | |     Bowled ........................ | |
| ........................ | |     Caught ........................ | |
| Catches ........................ | |     Caught & Bowled ........................ | |
| Run out ........................ | |     L.B.W. ........................ | |
| *Stumped ........................ | |     Other ........................ | |
| *Byes ........................ | | | |
| *If Keeping Wicket | | Total Number of Bowlers ........ | |

## NOTES

Weather and Effect on Game

Injuries

Other Useful Notes

Date ........................................20..... v. ....................................... C.C. Home/Away
League ................................. Division ............ Overs ............ Players ...............

## TEAM RESULT:

Won/Lost/Drawn by .................. Runs/by ................. Wickets .................. Points
Our Runs ............... Wickets ................ Their Runs ............... Wickets ...............

## PERSONAL RECORD

| Batting | Rating | Bowling | Rating |
|---|---|---|---|

**Batting** | **Rating**
Batting Order ........................................
Runs ....................................................
Number of 6's ......................................
Number of 4's ......................................
Wicket Partnership .............................
    Name ..........................................
    Runs ...........................................
Number of Overs .................................
Number balls faced ............................
How out ..............................................

**Fielding**
Main Positions ....................................
........................................
Catches ...............................................
Run out ................................................
*Stumped ...........................................
*Byes ...................................................
*If Keeping Wicket

**Bowling** | **Rating**
Number of Overs ...............................
Maiden Overs ....................................
Wickets ...............................................
Runs ....................................................
Extras ..................................................
    No Balls ......................................
    Wides ...........................................
    Byes .............................................
    Leg Byes .....................................
Bowling Average ...............................
Analysis of Wickets Taken ................
    Bowled ........................................
    Caught .........................................
    Caught & Bowled ........................
    L.B.W. ..........................................
    Other ............................................

Total Number of Bowlers ...................

## NOTES

Weather and Effect on Game

Injuries

Other Useful Notes

## NOTES ON SELECTED OPPONENTS — BATSMEN

| Date | Team | Name | How Wicket Lost | Runs | Notes |
|---|---|---|---|---|---|
|  |  |  |  |  |  |
|  |  |  |  |  |  |
|  |  |  |  |  |  |
|  |  |  |  |  |  |
|  |  |  |  |  |  |
|  |  |  |  |  |  |
|  |  |  |  |  |  |
|  |  |  |  |  |  |
|  |  |  |  |  |  |
|  |  |  |  |  |  |
|  |  |  |  |  |  |
|  |  |  |  |  |  |

# NOTES ON SELECTED OPPONENTS — BATSMEN

| Date | Team | Name | How Wicket Lost | Runs | Notes |
|------|------|------|-----------------|------|-------|
|      |      |      |                 |      |       |
|      |      |      |                 |      |       |
|      |      |      |                 |      |       |
|      |      |      |                 |      |       |
|      |      |      |                 |      |       |
|      |      |      |                 |      |       |
|      |      |      |                 |      |       |
|      |      |      |                 |      |       |
|      |      |      |                 |      |       |
|      |      |      |                 |      |       |
|      |      |      |                 |      |       |

# NOTES ON SELECTED OPPONENTS — BOWLERS

| Date | Team | Name | Bowling Style | How Wickets Taken | No. of Wickets | Notes |
|------|------|------|---------------|-------------------|----------------|-------|
|      |      |      |               |                   |                |       |
|      |      |      |               |                   |                |       |
|      |      |      |               |                   |                |       |
|      |      |      |               |                   |                |       |
|      |      |      |               |                   |                |       |
|      |      |      |               |                   |                |       |
|      |      |      |               |                   |                |       |
|      |      |      |               |                   |                |       |
|      |      |      |               |                   |                |       |
|      |      |      |               |                   |                |       |
|      |      |      |               |                   |                |       |
|      |      |      |               |                   |                |       |

# NOTES ON SELECTED OPPONENTS — BOWLERS

| Date | Team | Name | Bowling Style | How Wickets Taken | No. of Wickets | Notes |
|------|------|------|---------------|-------------------|----------------|-------|
|      |      |      |               |                   |                |       |
|      |      |      |               |                   |                |       |
|      |      |      |               |                   |                |       |
|      |      |      |               |                   |                |       |
|      |      |      |               |                   |                |       |
|      |      |      |               |                   |                |       |
|      |      |      |               |                   |                |       |
|      |      |      |               |                   |                |       |
|      |      |      |               |                   |                |       |
|      |      |      |               |                   |                |       |
|      |      |      |               |                   |                |       |
|      |      |      |               |                   |                |       |

# SEASON'S PERFORMANCE

| Against | Batting ||||| Bowling ||||| Fielding ||
| --- | --- | --- | --- | --- | --- | --- | --- | --- | --- | --- | --- |
| | Runs | 6's | 4's | Not Out | Overs | Maidens | Wickets | Runs | Average | Wickets | Rating* |
| | | | | | | | | | | | |
| | | | | | | | | | | | |
| | | | | | | | | | | | |
| | | | | | | | | | | | |
| | | | | | | | | | | | |
| | | | | | | | | | | | |
| | | | | | | | | | | | |
| | | | | | | | | | | | |
| | | | | | | | | | | | |
| | | | | | | | | | | | |
| | | | | | | | | | | | |
| | | | | | | | | | | | |
| | | | | | | | | | | | |

Carried Forward

*Rating* — Rate your games 1 = Best Game, etc.

# SEASON'S PERFORMANCE

| Against | Batting ||||| Bowling |||| Fielding ||
|---|---|---|---|---|---|---|---|---|---|---|---|
| | Runs | 6's | 4's | Not Out | Overs | Maidens | Wickets | Runs | Average | Wickets | Rating* |
| Brought Forward | | | | | | | | | | | |

|  |  |  |  |  |  |  |  |  |  |  |  |  |
|---|---|---|---|---|---|---|---|---|---|---|---|---|
|  |  |  |  |  |  |  |  |  |  |  |  |  |
|  |  |  |  |  |  |  |  |  |  |  |  |  |
|  |  |  |  |  |  |  |  |  |  |  |  |  |
|  |  |  |  |  |  |  |  |  |  |  |  |  |
|  |  |  |  |  |  |  |  |  |  |  |  |  |
|  |  |  |  |  |  |  |  |  |  |  |  |  |
|  |  |  |  |  |  |  |  |  |  |  |  |  |
|  |  |  |  |  |  |  |  |  |  |  |  |  |
|  |  |  |  |  |  |  |  |  |  |  |  | TOTAL |
|  |  |  |  |  |  |  |  |  |  |  |  | AVERAGES |

*Rating* — Rate your games 1 = Best Game, etc.

# TEAM RANKINGS FOR SEASON

| Ranking | BATTING |||  BOWLING |||  FIELDING |||
| --- | --- | --- | --- | --- | --- | --- | --- | --- | --- |
| | Name | Total Runs | Average | Name | Total Wickets | Average | Name | Wickets | Average |
| 1 | | | | | | | | | |
| 2 | | | | | | | | | |
| 3 | | | | | | | | | |
| 4 | | | | | | | | | |
| 5 | | | | | | | | | |
| 6 | | | | | | | | | |
| 7 | | | | | | | | | |
| 8 | | | | | | | | | |
| 9 | | | | | | | | | |
| 10 | | | | | | | | | |
| 11 | | | | | | | | | |
| 12 | | | | | | | | | |